The Butterfield Overland Mail Route Through New Mexico and Arizona 1858-1861

©2013 Kirby Sanders

- First edition April, 2013 -

Published by the author via Amazon CreateSpace
ISBN: 1484008502
ISBN 13: 978-1484008508

ACKNOWLEDGEMENTS

Particular thanks are due to Mr. Frank Norris and Mr. Aaron Mahr for shepherding me through the National Park Service processes and protocols. A second round of thanks to Mr. Norris for his technical editing assistance and erudite questions for clarification in the preparation of the reports. The numbers of individual local researchers who assisted by answering questions about their specific areas are too numerous to mention. However, special notice and thanks are due to authors Gerald Ahnert and George Hackler as well as researchers Don & Paul Matt, Fred Yeck, Chris Wray and other members of the Oregon-California Trails Association and the Santa Clarita Valley (CA) Historical Society. Also many thanks to my Arkansas trail buddy Scott Mashburn and to Marilyn Heifner, John McLarty, Glenn Jones and all of the members of the Heritage Trail Partners organization in Northwest Arkansas. Note to Glenn – "never trust a man with a ponytail."

CONTENTS

Author's Foreword ~ How To Use This Book   1

1 Introduction and Historical Background   3

2 El Paso (Texas) to Cottonwoods Ranch (New Mexico)   20

3 Cottonwoods Ranch to Fort Fillmore   27

4 Fort Fillmore to Mesilla   32

5 Mesilla to Picacho Pass   39

6 Picacho Pass to Cooke's Spring   44

7 Cooke's Spring to Cow Spring   51

8 Cow Spring to Soldiers' Farewell Hill   57

9 Soldiers' Farewell Hill to Mexican Springs / Shakespeare 63

10 Mexican Springs / Shakespeare to Steins Pass   69

11 Steins Pass (New Mexico) to Apache Springs (Arizona) 74

Apache Springs to Ewell's Spring   80

Ewell's Spring to Dragoon Spring   86

Dragoon Spring to San Pedro Station   91

San Pedro Station to Cienega Creek Crossing   99

Cienega Creek Crossing to Tucson   103

Tucson to Picacho Pass   108

Picacho Pass to Sacaton   115

Sacaton to Maricopa Wells   121

Maricopa Wells to Gila Ranch   127

Gila Ranch to Oatman Flat   135

Oatman Flat to Flapjack Ranch   142

Flapjack Ranch to Griswell's Station   148

Griswell's Station to Peterman's Station   152

Peterman's Station to Filibuster Camp   156

Filibuster Camp to Swiveller's Ranch   162

Swiveller's Ranch (Arizona) to Fort Yuma (California)   168

AUTHOR'S FOREWORD ~ HOW TO USE THIS BOOK

During 2010 and 2011, I was selected and tasked by the U.S. National Park Service (NPS) to prepare a preliminary series of reports and maps delineating the routes and known or presumed station locations used by the Butterfield Overland Mail Company for the first overland transcontinental mail service in American history. Said reports were to be included in an overall Special Resource Study to determine the eligibility of and potential for establishing the Butterfield route as a recognized National Trail under the administration and jurisdiction of NPS. The overall study and my portion thereof were mandated by order of Congress and signed into law by President Barack Obama under auspices of the Omnibus Public Lands Act of 2009.

The result of this work was eight hundred eighty-nine (889) pages of reports and documentation along with one hundred seventy-five (175) accompanying maps. What follows here are the resulting documents as filed with the NPS.

The work was to be a bibliographic study to establish the routes and stations as nearly as possible given existing research. It is hoped that the National Trail designation will be approved and that future additional research on the ground will result in a final and specific understanding and mapping of the entire route.

Given the volume of the reports, I have broken them out into several books that will cover the seven states involved in the study -- Missouri, Arkansas, Oklahoma, Texas, New Mexico, Arizona and California.

This volume will cover the route from El Paso, Texas through New Mexico and Arizona to the first station in California.

It should also be noted that in some cases, additional details have been discovered since the close of the NPS study period that have helped pin down or more accurately point toward certain station locations that had remained obscure. The effected reports have been annotated to update the most current information available as of this writing.

The maps contained in these reports were generated on a Google Maps base. Blue lines on maps indicate modern driving routes while red lines indicate the probable actual routes. Red lines only indicate the modern driving route approximates the actual route. Multi-colored lines indicate the likelihood of several different routes having been used at various times through the operation of the Butterfield stagecoaches. A digital database of the maps in this book has also been generated. The database maps contain driving directions for the recommended modern routes. For permission to access that database, contact the author via email at kirby.sanders.biz@gmail.com and an html format index including all seven states in the study will be provided.

Dates on the individual reports denote the date the report was prepared for submission to NPS. It should also be noted that these reports were intended as specific field-guide notes rather than for entertainment value.

2

INTRODUCTION AND HISTORICAL BACKGROUND
The Butterfield Overland Mail Ox-Bow Route
1858 - 1861
Prepared by Kirby Sanders for National Park Service
February 14, 2011

Purpose:

The purpose of this overall study is to establish a preliminary overview of the route and stations of the Butterfield Overland Mail Ox Bow Route (1858-1861) for use in preparation of the National Park Service Special Resource Study for the proposed Butterfield Overland Mail Ox Bow Route National Trail as mandated in Subtitle C; Section 7211 of the Omnibus Public Land Management Act of 2009 (Public Law 111-11).

Historical Significance:

The Butterfield Overland Mail Ox-Bow Route, for all that it was short-lived, has a well-deserved historical position behind its iconic stature in the lore of the American West and the popular culture that arose around it.

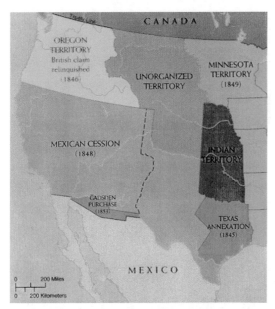

United States Territorial Acquisitions 1803 - 1853

The Butterfield Overland Mail represents a bold and important step toward unifying the United States as a nation whose territory had only recently spread "from sea to shining sea."

The Louisiana Purchase of 1803 brought 828,800 square miles of what is now the American Heartland into possession of the United States.

The annexation of the Republic of Texas in 1845 brought what is now the Lone Star State -- as well as parts of Colorado, Kansas, New Mexico, Oklahoma, and Wyoming.

By 1846, the relinquishment of the British to claims on the Oregon Territory filled in the Northwestern corner of the continental United States territory.

The Mexican Cession of California in 1848 pushed the boundary of the United States' lands south along the balance of the Pacific Coast and solidified the hold on the western and northern segments of the Texas claim.

Establishment of the Minnesota Territory in 1849 solidified the northern portion of the "Heartland." The Gadsden Purchase of 1853 filled in the last "piece of the puzzle" by establishing the definitive southern border of U.S. territory along the Rio Grande River in New Mexico and Arizona.

By the middle 1850s, the territory of the United States of America had expanded to what we now recognize as the "Continental U.S.", but it was hardly the coalition of states we recognize today. The State of Texas was recognized in its current form as of 1845. By 1850, what we now recognize as California had achieved statehood -- but much of the Intermountain West remained territorial -- sparsely settled and without the national representation that came with statehood.

"31 Star" Flag of the United States 1851 – 1858

By 1857 the midsection of the country was a gulf of territories separating the State of California from the other states.

Sixteen of what we now recognize as the "lower 48" states were territories rather than fully vested states. The present-day states of Minnesota, North Dakota, South Dakota, Nebraska, Kansas, Oklahoma, New Mexico, Colorado, Wyoming, Montana, Idaho, Utah, Arizona, Nevada, Oregon and Washington were all territories rather than fully vested states.

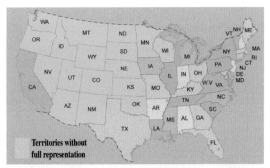

States and Territories of the United States as of 1857

Despite the territorial acquisitions that created a legitimate Continental United States, the 31 States and intervening Territories were not a nation that could readily communicate "from sea to shining sea".

Sending a simple letter or newspaper from New York to San Francisco during the mid-1850s could be accomplished one of three ways:

- by ship around the bottom of South America at Tierra Fuego,
- by ship to Panama for a (not always reliable) overland passage across the isthmus and north again by steamship, or
- by ship or riverboat to New Orleans for another ship's passage along the northern fringe of the Gulf of Mexico to Indianola TX for an overland journey to San Diego -- and another ship's passage onward to reach to San Francisco.

At best, one could expect one's letter or newspaper to arrive at its destination -- if it arrived at all -- within three months or so.

Socio-politically, by the mid-1850s, the "western states" (everything west of the Mississippi River -- Iowa, Missouri, Arkansas, Texas and California) as well as the southwestern territories were feeling "disconnected" as Americans. They were part of "one great nation" -- but could not easily get mail to or from family in the various eastern states. Meanwhile, rumblings in "the South" began to echo feelings of disenfranchisement as well -- but with far more dire talk of possible repercussions.

The 34th United States Congress responded with the passage of a postal act that required overland mail delivery by rail and coach between St. Louis MO and San Francisco CA via "the best valleys and passages" within 25 days -- which service should also accommodate passengers. That act also required that a reliable overland mail route connect the southern states to the west and southwest via Memphis TN.

Supporters of the project such as Senators William M. Gwin and John B. Weller (California) and Thomas J. Rusk (Texas) argued that their states and the territories deserved adequate mail service and that such service would help to spur settlement and economic development in the territories. Opponents generally argued that the Post Office should be self-supporting and that establishing the overland route would be too expensive to implement and had no promise of unsubsidized economic viability. Additionally, many of the Southern Senators felt the new service would favor the northern states with inadequate benefit to the South.

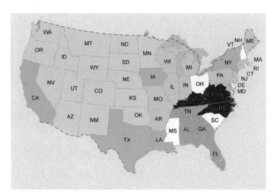

34th Senate vote on the 1857 Overland Mail Appropriation Bill

In February of 1857, the Senate approved the general plan for an overland mail service with a 24 - 10 vote as follows:
- California, Texas, Louisiana, Iowa, New York (two yea votes each)
- Arkansas, Missouri, Illinois, Wisconsin, Indiana, Michigan, Pennsylvania, Maryland, New Jersey, Connecticut, Massachusetts, Maine (one yea vote, one not voting)
- Kentucky, Virginia, North Carolina (two nay votes)
- Tennessee, Alabama, Georgia, Florida (one nay vote, one not voting)
- Mississippi, South Carolina, Ohio, Delaware, Rhode Island, New Hampshire (neither Senator voted).

It is interesting to note that none of the states split with a one yea / one nay vote.

The House of Representatives, however, did not pass the postal appropriation-- instead sending the bill to joint committee for further amendment. A House / Senate compromise bill was eventually approved and the basic Overland Mail bill was passed in September of 1857.

Enter John Butterfield and the Overland Mail Company. Butterfield was a successful (and politically well-connected) stagecoach and freight operator in New York and founder of the American Express Company. In conjunction with western partners Henry Wells and William G. Fargo (Wells Fargo Company), the Overland Mail Company was formed in 1857 and registered three of the nine operating proposals that were filed with Postmaster General Aaron V. Brown (a former governor of Tennessee).

Brown required that the Overland Mail Route be established "from St. Louis, Missouri, and from Memphis, Tennessee, converging at Little Rock, Arkansas; thence via Preston, Texas, or as nearly so as may be found advisable, to the best point of crossing the Rio Grande above El Paso and not far from Fort Fillmore (NM); thence, along the new road being opened and constructed under the direction of the Secretary of the Interior, to Fort Yuma, California; thence through the best passes and along the best valleys for safe and expeditious staging, to San Francisco."

On September 16, 1857 the Overland Mail Company was awarded a six year contract for operation of the postal route with service to begin in September 1858.

While none of the bids followed his route exactly, Postmaster General Brown selected one of the three Butterfield proposals with agreement that the basic route outline be followed with latitude for minor revisions on Butterfield's part in the interests of "safety, speed of mail and passenger delivery and reliability of roads." It is important to note, given this agreement, that the final Butterfield Overland Route from Memphis bypassed both Little Rock AR and Preston TX.

It is also important to note that the establishment of the Memphis to Ft. Smith route placated some of the southern objections by assuring the southern states that they would have convenient service -- although the people of Little Rock AR were never happy with the fact that they were bypassed. That bypass is a point of historical controversy to this day.

Initially, Little Rock was identified as an important potential hub at the convergence of the two routes originating from Saint Louis and Memphis. Unfortunately for Little Rock, the swampy terrain between Memphis and Little Rock barred a functional overland road between the two cities, erratic water levels on the connecting watercourses made steamboat traffic unreliable and the failure of the Memphis - Little Rock Railroad to complete through tracks between the two cities rendered an unworkable route by any conveyance from Memphis to Little Rock.

Butterfield effected a "fix" to this problem by following ground and ridge lines along the 1830s Military Road and continued well to the north of Little Rock. This shift along the Memphis - West road established the convergence of the two legs of the Butterfield Route at Fort Smith AR rather than Little Rock.

Thus the route was fixed -- traveling through the States (and Territories) of Missouri, Arkansas, Oklahoma, Texas, New Mexico, Arizona and California.

Establishing the Butterfield Route in Modern Terms

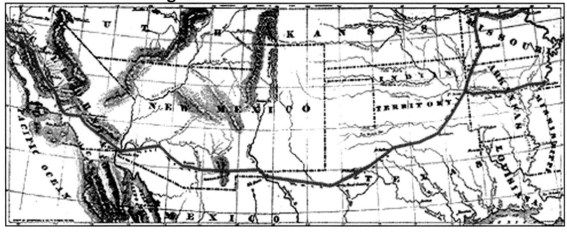

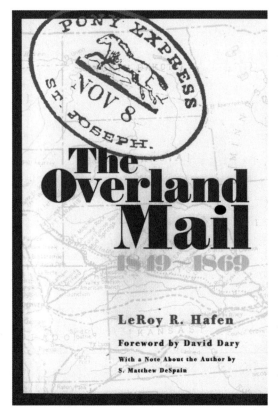

For historical background and sociopolitical overview, there are two primary studies that must be considered -- Leroy R. Hafen's *The Overland Mail, 1849-1869: Promoter of Settlement, Precursor of Railroads* (original publication by A. H. Clarke Company, 1926; Cleveland OH; Republished by University of Oklahoma Press; Norman OK, 2004) and Walter B. Lang's volumes *The First Overland Main Butterfield Trail St. Louis to San Francisco 1858-1861* and *The First Overland Mail, Butterfield Trail, San Francisco to Memphis, 1858-1861* (published by Roycrofters; East Aurora, New York, 1945).

Hafen is an excellent analysis of the sociopolitical background. Lang's work consists mainly of collected contemporaneous travelers' journals and news articles and is more valuable as a resource for the preparation of interpretive materials than for route identification.

Establishing the Butterfield Route in modern terms is not without some challenges as no other effort to track the entire route has been attempted for several decades. Much of the bibliographic data outlining the Butterfield Route is either out-of-date in terms of modern roads and / or out-of-print.

There are two primary contemporary reports that recount the entire Butterfield route in 1858. The first of those is the account of Waterman L. Ormsby. Ormsby was correspondent for the *New York Herald* newspaper who traveled the entire Butterfield route on its first westbound trip in 1858 and filed dispatches published in *the Herald*.

The second is a report by Goddard Bailey, a postal inspector who made the first eastbound trip and reported the point-to-point mileage between stations to Postmaster General Aaron V. Brown.

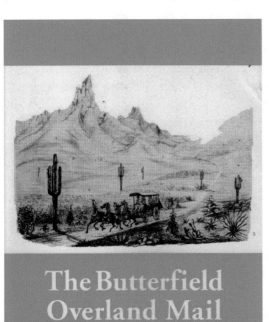

Ormsby's account mentions several identifiable landmarks along the route (although he does not specifically mention all of the stations) while Bailey gives an exact inventory of the stations and the miles between them.

Ormsby's account has been published and remains in-print (*The Butterfield Overland Mail - Only Through Passenger on the First Westbound Stage*; original publications New York Herald (NY) Sep 26 - Nov 19, 1858; republished by Henry E. Huntington Library and Art Gallery, San Marino CA, 1942 - 1998).

Bailey's itinerary was widely published in newspapers at the time (including the *New York Times*). His full report was also published in *De Bow's Review and Industrial Resources, Statistics etc*; (New Orleans and Washington City; 1858).

During the 1930s, Roscoe P. and Margaret B. Conkling used the Bailey and Ormsby data to plot and travel the 1858 Butterfield Route and documented several later station locations (1859-1861) as well.

Their research is now out-of-print, but was published (*The Butterfield Overland Mail, 1857–1869*; Three Volumes; Glendale, CA: A. H. Clark Company, 1947.) Full three-volume sets are now hard to come by and generally very expensive when they can be found.

The Conklings' research became the foundational resource for many subsequent Butterfield research efforts.

Unfortunately, however, many of the roads traveled by the Conklings in the 1930s have also become difficult (if not impossible) to discover --

rendering it often difficult to translate their route descriptions into modern terms.

Additionally, as local historians, later scholars and agencies have tracked the Butterfield Route in the ensuing years; some have faulted the Conklings' accuracy and methodology. The most frequent criticism in situations where additional findings do not mesh with the Conklings is that the Conklings relied on deductive processes to establish their routings and oral history interviews with site claimants as of the 1930s to establish station sites, but failed to adequately verify their conclusions and interviewees' statements to historical maps and records.

Throughout the preparation of this study, the Conklings have been used and cited as a foundational resource. Their dedication and years of work should be respected and honored, but not necessarily sanctified. For the purposes of this study, the Conklings have been considered to be a resource for equal consideration, but not the final word.

There was a national Butterfield Centennial recognition organized state-by-state in conjunction with the United States Post Office in 1958, however the information gathered by the State Committees does not appear to have been centralized. Additionally, records and reports from the state committees are sometimes difficult to come by and vary greatly in the amount of detail they contain. The records from the State of Oklahoma are well-detailed, excellent resources. The Arkansas report is rather brief and very general -- particularly regarding much of the Memphis to Ft. Smith Route.

It should be noted that the Missouri Butterfield Centennial Committee erected markers at each of the Butterfield Station locations in Missouri, most of which have been documented by Donald Mincke (*Chasing the Butterfield Overland Mail Stage -- A Road Guide Following the old Stage Route Across Missouri and Arkansas*). To date, however, no records of reports by that Committee or inventory of the markers have been located within the archives of the State Historical Society of Missouri.

To date, no archive of Centennial Committee reports have been located from the states of Texas, New Mexico, Arizona or California.

The National Coordinator of the 1958 Butterfield Centennial effort was one Vernon Brown of Tulsa OK. Archives of the National Postal Museum in Washington DC contain a telegram from President Dwight David Eisenhower recognizing Mr. Brown's efforts as coordinator and the Butterfield Centennial project overall. Once again, however, neither the Postal Museum nor the Oklahoma Historical Society are in possession of Mr. Brown's notes and papers. Neither are they aware of where such collection might be -- or even if such a collection exists.

After the 1958 Butterfield Centennial effort, study of the Butterfield Route "went fallow" on the national front. It fell to individual authors and local /

regional historical preservation organizations, genealogical societies and museums to be the "keepers of the flame" for the Butterfield Route.

Methodology in Establishing the Butterfield Stations and Landmarks in Modern Terms

OVERLAND MAIL COMPANY.
THROUGH TIME SCHEDULE BETWEEN
ST. LOUIS, MO., MEMPHIS, TENN. } & SAN FRANCISCO, CAL.
[Sep. 16th, 1858.

GOING WEST. / GOING EAST.

LEAVE.	DAYS.	Hour.	Miles. Place	Time allowed.	Av'ge Miles per Hour.	LEAVE.	DAYS.	Hour.	Miles. Place	Time allowed.	Av'ge Miles per Hour.
St. Louis, Mo., & Memphis, Tenn.	Every Monday & Thursday,	8.00 A.M				San Francisco, Cal.	Every Monday & Thursday,	8.00 A.M			
P. R. R. Terminus, "	" Monday & Thursday,	6.00 P.M	160	10	16	Firebaugh's Ferry, "	" Tuesday & Friday,	11.00 A.M	163	27	6
Springfield, "	" Wednesday & Saturday,	7.45 A.M	143	37¾	3⅝	Visalia, "	" Wednesday & Saturday,	5.00 A.M	82	18	4½
Fayetteville, "	" Thursday & Sunday,	10.15 A.M	100	26½	3½	Ft. Tejon, (Via Los Angeles)	" Thursday & Sunday,	9.00 A.M	127	28	4½
Fort Smith, Ark.	" Friday & Monday,	3.30 A.M	65	17½	3⅝	San Bernardino, "	" Friday & Monday,	5.30 P.M	150	32½	4½
Sherman, Texas	" Sunday & Wednesday,	12.30 A.M	205	45	4½	Fort Yuma, "	" Sunday & Wednesday,	1.30 P.M	200	44	4½
Fort Belknap. "	" Monday & Thursday,	9.00 A.M	146½	32½	4½	Gila River,* Arizona	" Monday & Thursday,	7.30 P.M	135	30	4½
Fort Chadbourn, "	" Tuesday & Friday,	3.15 P.M	136	30½	4½	Tucson, "	" Wednesday & Saturday	3.00 A.M	141	31½	4½
Pecos River, (Em. Crossing)	" Thursday & Sunday,	3.45 A.M	165	36½	4½	Soldier's Farewell. "	" Thursday & Sunday,	8.00 P.M	184½	41	4½
El Paso, "	" Saturday & Tuesday,	11.00 A.M	248½	55¼	4½	El Paso, Tex.	" Saturday & Tuesday,	5.30 A.M	150	33½	4½
Soldier's Farewell "	" Sunday & Wednesday,	8.30 P.M	150	33½	4½	Pecos River, (Em. Crossing)	" Monday & Thursday	12.45 P.M	248½	55½	4½
Tucson, Arizona	" Tuesday & Friday,	1.30 P.M	184½	41	4½	Fort Chadbourn, "	" Wednesday & Saturday	1.15 A.M	165	36½	4½
Gila River,* "	" Wednesday & Saturday	9.00 P.M	141	31½	4½	Fort Belknap, "	" Thursday & Sunday,	7.30 A.M	136	30½	4½
Fort Yuma, Cal.	" Friday & Monday,	3.00 A.M	135	30	4½	Sherman, "	" Friday & Monday,	4.00 P.M	146½	32½	4½
San Bernardino "	" Saturday & Tuesday,	11.00 P.M	200	44	4½	Fort Smith, Ark.	" Sunday & Wednesday,	1.00 P.M	205	45	4½
Ft. Tejon, (Via Los Angeles)	" Monday & Thursday,	7.30 A.M	150	32½	4½	Fayetteville, Mo.	" Monday, & Thursday,	6.15 A.M	65	17½	3½
Visalia, "	" Tuesday & Friday,	11.30 A.M	127	28	4½	Springfield, "	" Tuesday & Friday,	8.45 A.M	100	26½	3½
Firebaugh's Ferry, "	" Wednesday & Saturday,	5.30 A.M	82	18	4½	P. R. R. Terminus, "	" Wednesday & Saturday	10.30 P.M	143	37½	3½
(Arrive) San Francisco, "	" Thursday & Sunday,	8.30 A.M	163	27	6	(Arrive) St. Louis, Mo., & Memphis, Tenn. }	" Thursday & Sunday,		160	10	16

This Schedule may not be exact—Superintendents, Agents, Station-men, Conductors, Drivers and all employees are particularly directed to use every possible exertion to get the Stages through in quick time, even though they may be ahead of this time.
If they are behind this time, it will be necessary to urge the animals on to the highest speed they can be driven without injury.
Remember that no allowance is made in the time for ferries, changing teams, &c. It is therefore necessary that each driver increase his speed over the average per hour enough to gain the necessary time for meals, changing teams, crossing ferries, &c.
Every person in the Company's employ will always bear in mind that each minute of time is of importance. If each driver on the route loses fifteen (15) minutes, it would make a total loss of time, on the entire route, of twenty-five (25) hours, or, more than one day. If each one loses ten (10) minutes it would make a total loss of sixteen and one half (16½) hours, or, the best part of a day.
On the contrary, if each driver gains that amount of time, it leaves a margin of time against accidents and extra delays.
All hands will see the great necessity of promptness and dispatch: every minute of time is valuable as the Company are under heavy forfeit if the mail is behind time.
Conductors must note the hour and date of departure from Stations, the causes of delay, if any, and all particulars. They must also report the same fully to their respective Superintendents.

* The Station referred to on Gila River, is 40 miles west of Maricopa Wells.

JOHN BUTTERFIELD.
Pres't.

Butterfield Schedule and Timetable as published by the Overland Mail Company, 1858

Many of the bibliographic resources that have been most helpful in locating the modern sites of the various Butterfield Stations are either privately published by the authors themselves, published by small and / or academic publishing houses or held in the archives of State Historical Societies or local museums. Of particular note for their modern regional or state research efforts are:
   • Donald Mincke (Missouri and Arkansas)
   • A.C. Greene (Texas)
   • Don and Paul Matt (Missouri, Arkansas, Oklahoma and Texas)
   • George Hackler (New Mexico)
   • Gerald Ahnert (Arizona)
   • Dan Talbot (Arizona)
In 2008, Casey Gill (curator of the Wells Fargo History Museum in San Diego CA) recreated the approximate route of the Butterfield from Saint Louis to San Francisco along modern roads in a recreational vehicle as part of the

Wells Fargo Company's Butterfield Sesquicentennial recognition. Notes from his travels were posted to an Internet blog describing his journey.

Four of the regional offices of the Texas Heritage Trails Program have also been active in recent Butterfield Overland Mail research and should be more closely consulted for future Planning and Implementation / Interpretive projects. Those offices are the Lakes Trail Region located in Granbury, Fort Trail Region located in Abilene, the Pecos Trail Region located in Sonora, and the Mountain Trail Region located in Van Horn. The Lakes Trail Region has been particularly active in ongoing Butterfield Research.

The recent emergence of "geocaching" as a hobby has led to the establishment of numerous small Internet websites and "blogs" that contain helpful information regarding various Butterfield Station sites and related historical markers on the local level. With the modern availability of relatively inexpensive GPS devices, numerous local hobbyists have taken to logging the latitude and longitude coordinates of historical sites in their immediate neighborhoods on individual internet websites -- resulting in numerous widely scattered small resources for locating individual Butterfield-related sites.

The efforts of these amateur sleuths is commendable and should be taken into account -- although the quality of reporting is sometimes uneven.

Of particular merit in this arena is a website established by William Nienke and Sam Morrow in conjunction with the Texas Geocaching Association. That website contains a searchable database of latitude and longitude coordinates for most of the historical markers in Texas.

Of final note regarding the establishment of coordinates for Butterfield-related station sites, landmarks and relevant historical markers is the fact that many of the bibliographic resources (particularly those published in the 1930s through the 1950s) established the locations of the Butterfield Station sites by notation of Township, Range and Section description. In many cases, some of the more obscure station sites can be approximated in terms of latitude and longitude by converting and mapping the corners and centroid of those Township / Range / Section descriptions to determine approximate latitude and longitude soordinates for individual sites.

In some few cases, the actual station sites have been obscured (or obliterated) by time and progress. In those cases, the station locations have been approximated according to Bailey's mileages along the known route from the last known point, reputable modern research and (where they have been discovered) Civil War records. These obscured or approximated locations have been so noted in the narrative reports.

It should also be noted that there are occasional "spurious" reports of purported "Butterfield Stations" near (but not on) the documentable

Butterfield Route. These cases do not seem to be malicious in intent. Generally they can be traced to post-contemporary diary entries that fail to take into account that the actual Butterfield Route may have been 20 or so miles distant -- and the actual stage that served a given community was a local or connecting trunk line operated by an independent carrier.

Granted -- there has come to be a certain romance to a "Butterfield connection," in the popular culture but in many cases these spurious claims appear to be a matter of misinterpretation of early diary entries.

Methodology in Establishing the Original Route in Modern Terms

The Overland Mail Company did not forge 3,000-plus miles of new trails and roads to establish their route as of 1858.

In mapping the approximate original Butterfield Route, contemporaneous route descriptions were compared to later field research (where available) -- always bearing In mind Postmaster General A.V. Brown's specific instructions in 1857:

> "from St. Louis, Missouri, and from Memphis, Tennessee, converging at Little Rock, Arkansas; thence via Preston, Texas, or as nearly so as may be found advisable, to the best point of crossing the Rio Grande above El Paso and not far from Fort Fillmore (NM); thence, along the new road being opened and constructed under the direction of the Secretary of the Interior, to Fort Yuma, California; thence through the best passes and along the best valleys for safe and expeditious staging, to San Francisco."

For the most part, the Butterfield Route connected several known roads -- in keeping with Postmaster Brown's instructions.

• In Missouri, the Butterfield Route originated by rail on the Pacific Railroad from St. Louis to Tipton MO and then Syracuse MO before tracking known local roads southward to Arkansas.

• Through western Arkansas, the route again tracked known local roads as well as those forged by the military in establishing the boundary with Indian Territory during the 1830s and 1840s as well as portions of the Trail of Tears routes used by the U.S. military during the Indian relocation movements of the 1830s. On the Memphis to Fort Smith leg, the Butterfield Route essentially tracks the Military Road established to link those two settlements in the late 1830s - early 1840s.

• Through Oklahoma and into Texas, The Butterfield Route followed documented Choctaw Nation roads established after the relocation of 1830 into the historic "Texas Road" / Osage Trace that was the main emigrant route and Military Road from Fort Gibson, Kansas to Texas predating the Butterfield.

• As a general reference, much of the Butterfield route roughly traced roads described by Randolph Barnes Marcy from Fort Smith AR to Dona Ana

NM in the 1840s (published as *The Prairie Traveler - A Handbook for Overland Expeditions*; New York; Harper & Brothers; 1859).

• In Northeast and North Central Texas, the Butterfield route diverged from Marcy's 1849 expedition route but appears to roughly track other trails identified by Marcy during another expedition through Texas in 1854.

• Through western New Mexico and Arizona, the Butterfield Route tracks routes identified by John Russell Bartlett (1850-1853) during his survey as Boundary Commissioner to establish the U.S. / Mexico border in conjunction with negotiation of the Gadsden Purchase (published in *Personal Narrative of Explorations and Incidents in Texas, New Mexico, California, Sonora and Chihuahua*; D. Appleton and Company; New York; 1854). This route also follows sections of the Mormon Battalion route from Kanesville (Council Bluffs) IA to San Diego CA (1846-1847).

• In western Arizona and into Southern California, the Butterfield Route substantially tracked the early route of the Juan Bautista de Anza expedition (1774), as did Bartlett.

• Into Central and Northern California, the Butterfield Route roughly tracks the de Anza (with some modifications) as well as the Camino Real / Mission Trail (1600s) and several local trails that connected gold camps and settlements established by the "49ers".

There are also historical maps available for each state dating from the early 1850s that help to identify what later became the Butterfield Route. Another excellent resource for Texas and New Mexico is the *Map of Texas and Parts of New Mexico* published in 1857 by the United States War Department Topographical Engineers. Additionally, several maps from the *Official Records Atlas of the Union and Confederate Armies* (1873) help to identify various Butterfield route segments and locations that were near or relevant to Civil War troop movements and encampments.

Ormsby contains some route descriptions and approximated mileages. Lang has transcribed several other contemporaneous reports that describe and give approximated mileages for a scattering of station locations.

Given that Postal Inspector Goddard Bailey's report to Postmaster General Brown was the "official word" on the itinerary and mileages in 1858; this author felt it most prudent and reliable to compare Ormsby, the Lang transcriptions and modern data to Bailey's mileage reports in setting a foundation for actual routes. It should be noted that the coaches ridden by Bailey were outfitted with an early version of an odometer (attached to a rear wheel of the coach) so as to render a "true" reading of the mileages for his official report to the Postmaster. For this reason, Bailey's measurements have been considered to be the most reliable "scientific data" as of 1858.

Where Ormsby and other journalistic chroniclers stated mileages that differed from (or were not measured by) Bailey, said data has been included in the reports -- but the journalists generally relied on the word of the drivers that the distance from "Station A" to "Station B" was a given number of miles.

Comparison of all of the early maps and reports helps to establish the Butterfield Route when these established earlier routes are aligned to Bailey's mileages and Ormsby's narratives. Further, comparing all of the early data to modern terrain maps and the array of modern Township / Range or GPS / geocache data and writings establishes reliable approximations of the original Butterfield Route.

Current satellite map overlays, terrain maps and topographic maps were then compared to Bailey's mileages, the known station locations and the modern field research to discover "the best roads and valleys" through a given area as the early data was overlaid onto modern maps.

Given these parameters and resources, the overall Butterfield Overland Mail Route data was plotted "station by station" onto a series of approximately 200 mapped segments. Each identifiable station location, notable topographic location, geological landmark and many relevant state historical markers were plotted on the individual maps -- thus creating a series of identifiable "dots" to be connected.

Using that series of "dots", what was known of the route was plotted point-to-point given the specific terrain of a given area using Bailey's measured mileages as a guideline for what "should be" the distance of the route segment.

Where specific route descriptions have been offered according to contemporaneous reports, those descriptions have been included in the segment reports.

In other cases, local field research (1930s to present) has detailed the original route through much of the overall trail. Where that data has been discovered, it has been included in the individual segment reports. On the other hand, there are a few cases where there still appear to be more than one candidate for the optimum "original route". Those specific cases have been discussed in the individual segment reports.

In some instances where the originating station locations remain obscure, there may be a slight margin of error in the segment mapping. Those cases have been specifically detailed in the individual segment narrative reports.

Reliable modern data (1930s to present has) also been collected and published that helps to identify many of the segment routings.

State by state, the most reliable modern data and descriptions regarding the original Butterfield Route discovered to-date have been recorded by:

• Missouri and Arkansas: Donald Mincke - *Chasing the Butterfield Overland Mail Stage* (2005 - self-published)

• Oklahoma: *Butterfield Centennial Committee Report - Butterfield Overland Mail* (1958 - Chronicles of Oklahoma; Oklahoma Historical Society

• Texas: A. C. Greene - 900 Miles On the Butterfield Trail (1994 - University of North Texas Press)

    • New Mexico: George Hackler - *The Butterfield Trail in New Mexico* (2005 - Yucca Enterprises). Mr. Hackler also supplied a substantial amount of assistance and direction in establishing the segment routes and station sites in correspondence as of year 2010.

    • Arizona: Gerald Ahnert - *Retracing the Butterfield Overland Trail through Arizona; a Guide to the Route of 1857-1861* (1973 - Westernlore Press). Once again, Mr. Ahnert also supplied a substantial amount of assistance and direction in establishing the segment routes and station sites in correspondence as of year 2010. • Data update as of March, 2013 – Mr. Ahnert has also published an updated and revised study, *The Butterfield Trail and Overland Mail Company in Arizona; 1858-1861* (2011 – Canastota Publishing Co, Canastota NY).

    • Don Talbot - *Historical Guide to the Mormon Battalion and Butterfield Trail* (1992 - Western Lore Press)

California:

    • Chris Wray of the Oregon - California Trails Association (OCTA) supplied a substantial amount of unpublished data and assistance based upon recent mapping and GIS data gathered by OCTA mapping teams in Southern California (Pilot Knob / Andrade CA to Warner Ranch). Said data was also compared to existing information published regarding the National Park Service de Anza Trail.

    Through the Central Valley and into Northern California, the data appears to be more scattered. In that area, however, information establishing the early Camino Real and Mission Trail was used to verify the routes.

    Where possible, local / regional experts were contacted and interviewed regarding the route through their area. While the individual contributions of area residents, town / county museums and local genealogical societies are too numerous to mention; three individuals deserve particular mention for their assistance.

    In the preparation of these reports, draft copies of relevant reports and maps were reviewed by:

    • Gerald Ahnert - author *Retracing the Butterfield Overland Trail through Arizona; a Guide to the Route of 1857-186*, and *The Butterfield Trail and Overland Mail Company in Arizona; 1858-1861;*

    • George Hackler - author of *The Butterfield Trail in New Mexico;*

    • Chris Wray - the Oregon California Trails Association (southern California and Mexico, Pilot Knob CA to Warner Ranch CA).

    Where these individuals were contacted and comments received, their comments and suggestions were carefully considered and included in the resulting segment reports.

    Efforts were also made to enlist the direct assistance of

• Donald Mincke - author of *Chasing the Butterfield Overland Mail Stage* (deceased as of November 11, 2007),

• A. C. Greene - author *900 Miles On the Butterfield Trail* (deceased as of April 5, 2002),

• Don Talbot - *Historical Guide to the Mormon Battalion and Butterfield Trail* (unable to locate 2008 to-date).

Narrative Reports

Of the approximately 200 individual narrative reports - these have been written to establish the criteria used in the identification of each route segment and the placement of the sites themselves.

Each of these reports contains a limited amount of interpretive data regarding the various stations and landmarks. Where local museums, state and federal historic parks and other notable modern facilities became apparent along the route, such locations were noted on the maps and segment reports.

While additional interpretive data has been collected for many of the stations and route segments has been discovered (including an initial image library of historical photographs and sketches of station sites and landmarks as well as recent photographs of restored sites and relevant historical markers), that full data is not included in these report. The focus of these reports is on the Butterfield Route rather than full interpretive descriptions of every station, stationmaster and notable bump in the road.

Said additional interpretive data can be readily included in future Preservation Planning and Implementation efforts.

It should be noted that in a few instances, definitive station locations could not be determined and had to be approximated based upon Bailey's mileage reports, contemporaneous historical mention, local field data and other available information. In some other instances, the actual station locations have been inundated by the later construction of reservoirs, obliterated by flooding or demolished to make way for urban and agricultural development. In yet a few other instances, there is conflicting data -- different resources have cited different locations for a single station. These anomalies have been noted in the individual maps and segment reports.

All of this data has been supplied to National Park Service Intermountain Region office in Santa Fe NM.

Into the Future

As an organizational criterion, this study was prepared on the assumption that it is "Phase One" of what is essentially a three-phase process in establishing the Butterfield Overland Mail Ox Bow Route National Historic Trail or other NPS Master Preservation Plan.

Said three phases were assumed to be:

• Phase One - Preliminary Route Establishment (based upon bibliographic resources and maps data)

• Phase Two - Preservation Planning (public meetings to establish a nationwide cooperative research and reporting effort, additional field research; onsite GPS readings for station locations; expansion of cooperative research with state and local experts on the Butterfield; inventory and (where needed) inspection of local archives to develop a Butterfield Image Library & definitive inventory of interpretive resources and other activities that would definitively confirm or correct the preliminary data for station locations and trail routing and facilitate the development of interpretive materials)

• Phase Three - Preservation Implementation (review of cooperative research results, development of signage and other interpretive materials regarding the relevant station locations and the route itself; consultation with state, regional and local tourism boards, Chambers of Commerce, economic development boards and other stakeholders to promote benefits and use of the Trail.)

The foundational theory of this "Phase One" process was quite simple. In order to facilitate "Phase Two" field research, one has to initially determine where "the field" is.

While most of the Butterfield Overland Mail stations and other notable landmarks can be placed with relative certainty, it is expected that modern in-depth historical and archaeological research along each of the route segments ("Phase Two") will help to definitively "pin" most of the relevant sites as well as the route itself. It is expected that this additional research may result in updated latitude and longitude placement of some stations in the future as well as some shifts in the approximated route.

It is also expected that during Phase Two (Preservation Planning) and Phase Three (Preservation Implementation) will be -- as this Texas boy would say -- "cussed and discussed" to the point at which Federal, State and Local cooperation establishes a thoroughly accurate reflection of this important transit and communication corridor.

Conclusion

The purpose of this preliminary Special Resource Study was to establish a series of definitively identified latitude / longitude "starting points" that are joined by the most accurate route mapping possible given best-available bibliographic and mapping data to-date.

That preliminary goal has been achieved.

In some cases, we are on the brink of losing parts of this important connection to our Unity as a Nation forever. Only additional cooperative research that is organized in conjunction with local jurisdictions and accessible via a National Inventory and database of Butterfield related Sites and the establishment of a readily accessible central archive will help us avoid losing these pieces of our shared National Identity to historical obscurity.

From this point, I would urge the House of Representatives, the Senate, The President of the United States and the Secretary of the Interior to authorize, fund and appropriate the continued detailed local research and the implementation of a Butterfield Overland Mail Oxbow Route (1858-1861) National Historic Trail followed by the implementation of an appropriate Master Preservation Plan.

- Kirby Sanders -
February 14, 2011

• Update as of April 2013 • The individual segment reports as supplied to the National Park Service included the maps herein. Additional photographs were added during the preparation of this book.

El Paso (Texas) to Cottonwoods Ranch (New Mexico)

April 16, 2011

Franklin Station - El Paso, TX • El Paso County (N31° 45' 24.30", W106° 29' 19.32")

TO Cottonwoods Station NM - Berino, NM • Doña Ana County (N32° 4' 5.19", W106° 37' 15.08")

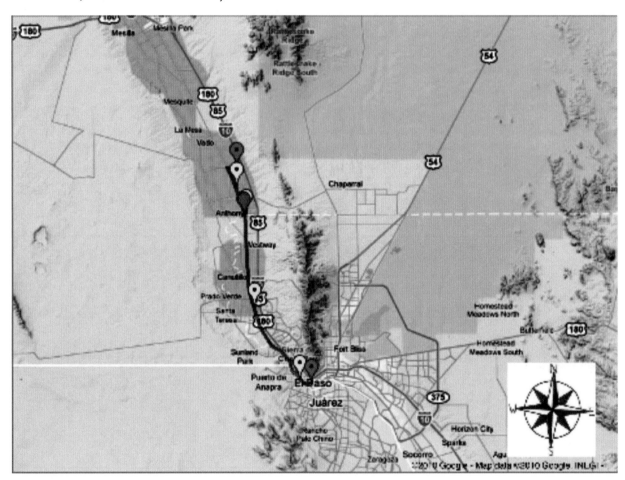

Approximate actual route Franklin Station (El Paso) to Cottonwoods Ranch 24.5 miles

(1858 Bailey Itinerary says 22, Ormsby says 21 miles)

Secondary Landmarks:

Camino Real Historical Marker - *Texas Historic Sites Atlas* #642 - 1720 W. Old Paisano, El Paso - N31° 45' 43.92", W106° 30' 34.94"

Camino Real Historical Marker - *Texas Historic Sites Atlas* #647 -5800 Doniphan Dr, El Paso - approximate coordinates N31 52' 01.85", W106 35' 20.16"

Cottonwoods Ranch site per Matt Brothers - La Tuna Federal Correctional Facility (TX) - approximate coordinates N31° 58' 51.42", W106° 35' 25.62"

Cottonwoods Ranch site (approximate) per Ormsby mileage - 200 block W Washington Street, Anthony NM - approximate coordinates N32° 0' 3.80", W106° 36' 31.51"

Cottonwoods Ranch site per Hackler - approximate coordinates N31 59' 52", W106 36' 30"

Cottonwoods Ranch site per Bailey (approximate) - 300 block Joy Drive near Monte Bello Road, Anthony NM - approximate coordinates N32° 2' 21.16", W106° 36' 54.45"

Notes:

Leaving Texas and entering New Mexico, the Butterfield route is fairly clear but there is conflicting data regarding the exact location of the next station at Cottonwoods Ranch.

Upon departing Franklin Station westward, the first several blocks of the route followed the "new" trail via El Paso as contemporary to the mid 1800s, (established by Marcy and Skillman, Wasson & Birch). This track then rejoined the Camino Real de Tierra Adentro Trail on the western verge of modern downtown in the vicinity of Oñate Crossing as identified the National Park Service (near intersection of W. Paisano Drive and W. Yandell Drive, approximate coordinates N31° 45 43.92", W106° 30 34.94").

Given the surrounding terrain, the route of earlier trails and most recent research, the Butterfield route out of El Paso then tracked northward along the valley between the western foot of the Franklin Mountains and the Rio Grande River -- essentially following the route of Texas Highway 20. Into New Mexico, the route continued along what is now New Mexico Highway 478.

This further route represents the known trail of the Spanish Camino Real de Tierra Adentro as well as the 1849 Marcy Route to Doña Ana and Bartlett's Texas-Mexico Boundary survey route. It is also quite clearly depicted on the 1857 War Department Topographical Engineers Map. This segment also represents a continuation along the route established by Skillman, Wasson, Birch et al. for the San Antonio - San Diego Line.

In modern terms, George Hackler and the Matt Brothers have investigated this segment.

Of assistance in tracking the Butterfield Route through this segment are two Texas historical markers identifying the early Camino Real to the west and north of El Paso.

The first of those markers (*Texas Historic Sites Atlas* #642 - erected 1983) is located at 1720 W. Old Paisano Road in El Paso (approximate coordinates per Nienke and Morrow N31° 45' 43.92", W106° 30' 34.94"). That marker (which is a repeat of other Texas markers along the Camino Real) reads "Camino Real - For more than 200 years the Camino Real, or Royal Road, was the major route for transporting commercial goods from Mexico City and Chihuahua to Santa Fe and Taos. First traveled by Juan de Oñate during his 1598 expedition to New Mexico, the Camino Real followed the San Elizario, Socorro, and Ysleta Road, crossed the Rio Grande west of present downtown El Paso, and continued north into New Mexico. When the Rio Grande was established as the U.S. - Mexico boundary in 1848, this section of the old Camino Real became part of the United States."

The second Camino Real marker (*Texas Historic Sites Atlas* #647 - erected 1983) is reported to be located at 5800 Doniphan Drive in El Paso. No text is listed for that marker, however. Nienke and Morrow also note this marker but show neither coordinates nor text. Using the street address as a key, approximate coordinates would be N31 52' 01.85", W106 35' 20.16".

As to the placement of the Cottonwoods Station per, the data gets confusing.

The Matt Brothers place the Cottonwoods Station site on the Texas side of the state boundary at La Tuna in Anthony TX. Specifically, they write "Cotton Wood Station - N31° 58.857' W106° 35.427' - is located 350 feet northwest of the Santa Fe railroad station at La Tuna. La Tuna is a Federal Correctional Facility. Advisedly, one should avoid that. We did."

Hackler places the Cottonwoods Station in the vicinity of Anthony, TX (approximate coordinates N31 59' 52", W106 36' 30"). He writes: "Henry Skillman, who drove the first westbound Butterfield stage into El Paso, had a house at Cottonwoods which served as a station. The location of the [Rio Grande] river in 1860 can be visualized by following the present New Mexico / Texas boundary south from the intersection with the 32nd Parallel. The [northbound] trail skirted to the northwest around Anthony and then headed east to the sandhills, an easier path than the bosque of the river bottom."

In a March, 2010, telephone interview, Hackler insisted that the Skillman property (and most likely the Cottonwoods Station) straddled the Texas / New Mexico boundary in the vicinity of Anthony TX / Anthony NM. (The town of Anthony lies on both sides of the border – partly within Texas and partly within New Mexico). He also noted, however, that his coordinates were keyed upon the location of Henry Skillman's **residence** in the area rather than a definitive finding of the Butterfield Station site.

Ormsby estimated the mileage from Franklin Station to Cottonwoods at 21 miles -- which would put the station site on the New Mexico side of the state boundary in the vicinity of the 200 block of W Washington Street in Anthony NM (approximate coordinates N32° 0' 3.80", W106° 36' 31.51"). That placement is slightly north of the Hackler location.

Bailey cites the mileage between Cottonwoods and Franklin as 22 miles -- which would place the station north of the Matt, Hackler and Ormsby coordinates in the vicinity of Joy Drive and Monte Bello Road (approximate coordinates N32° 2' 21.16", W106° 36' 54.45")

There are other reports, however, that seem to indicate the existing community of Berino (approximately six miles north of Anthony) as the likely Cottonwoods station location. This location for the likely Butterfield Station site more closely matches to the mileages cited by Ormsby and Bailey.

Greene notes that the Butterfield coaches **passed** through the area referred to as La Tuna (the Spanish name for prickly-pear cactus) at the Texas / New Mexico border en route to Cottonwoods Station.

Information from the Anthony - Berino Economic Development Council notes that "Anthony has long been the gateway of trade routes in the Southwest. The Butterfield Trail passed just north of Anthony and the Camino Real Trade Route from Mexico City passed directly through the community. "

New Mexico researcher Art Pike, in his *New Mexico Wanderings*, notes:

> "Berino is on NM 226 a mile east of NM 478 and about 3 miles west of Interstate 10 (the Interstate from Las Cruces to El Paso) in southwest United States. It's about 20 miles south of Las Cruces, still in Doña Ana County. It grew around a Butterfield Overland Stage station.

Originally it was located on the Cottonwoods Ranch northeast of Anthony, and on early maps was listed as Los Alamos, later translated to Cottonwoods, and even later to Berino or 'ford' in Spanish. West of Berino are the AT&SF railroad tracks in Berino Siding. Further west over the tracks and across the river is Chamberino, founded by folks from Berino seeking higher land to avoid Rio Grande floods."

James W. White in his 1997 *History of Doña Ana County Post Offices* concurs with Pike in placing Berino as Cottonwoods, writing:

"Berino is a small settlement on NM 226, one mile east of NM 478, and 19 miles south of Las Cruces. An old Hispanic settlement which means 'ford,' and is located near the east bank of the Rio Grande. A sister settlement is across the river and is also named Berino. The name may also be related to 'merino,' a breed of sheep. Reportedly, the settlement was once called Cottonwoods. The location of the settlement has shifted over time to the old RR siding of Berino. [Based on Robert Julyan, *The Place Names of New Mexico*.]

This small agricultural community was originally known as Cottonwood and was on the Butterfield Overland Mail Route. The settlement is located twenty miles south southeast of Las Cruces near the east bank of the Rio Grande. Berino is said to be an Indian word that means ford. The Berino Post Office was established on September 3, 1902. Aurilla Tadlock was the first postmaster and received the mail daily from the Railway Post Office (RPO) car on the Atchison, Topeka and Santa Fe Railroad."

Francis and Roberta Fugate's *Roadside History of New Mexico* notes that Berino "was cited on maps in 1851 as 'Los Alamos' and later translated to 'Cottonwoods'".

For the purpose of this report and given the preponderance of local information that has been found compared to Bailey and Ormsby's mileage reports, this report has landmarked the northernmost possibility for Cottonwoods Station at Berino NM.

References:

Anthony - Berino Economic Development Council; *Welcome to Anthony - Berino Economic Development*; Internet publication accessible at http://www.anthonynewmexico.org/ (accessed May 23, 2010)

Bailey, Goddard; *California -- Arrival of the Overland Mail -- Itinerary of the Route*; as reported by newspaper article; New York Times (NY) - October 14, 1858

Bailey, Goddard; *Report to Postmaster A.V. Brown - Full itinerary as reported by De Bow's Review and Industrial Resources, Statistics etc;* published by De Bow's Review; New Orleans and Washington City; 1858. See specifically *Internal Improvements - 1. Wagon Road to the Pacific*; pp 719-721. Internet accessible at http://books.google.com/books?id=5CYoAAAAYAAJ&pg=PA720&lpg=PA720&dq=Cienega+de+los+Pimas&source=bl&ots=_5lZw_Bq23&sig=T6scCb8cpbY7KwjxpYoNvZpcgvI&hl=en&ei=i6KnS6KNOIr2M5yprIED&sa=X&oi=book_result&ct=result&resnum=2&ved=0CAwQ6AEwAQ#v=onepage&q=Cienega%20de%20los%20Pimas&f=false (accessed March 22, 2010)

Bartlett, John Russell; *Personal Narrative of Explorations and Incidents in Texas, New Mexico, California, Sonora and Chihuahua - Vol. One*; D. Appleton and Company; *New York; 1854*

Conkling, Roscoe P. and Margaret B.; *The Butterfield Overland Mail, 1857–1869* (3 vols); Glendale, CA: A. H. Clark Company, 1947.

Fugate, Francis L. & Roberta B. Fugate; *Roadside History of New Mexico*; Mountain Press Publishing Company; Missoula MT; 1989

Greene, A.C.; *900 Miles On the Butterfield Trail*; University of North Texas Press; 1994

Hackler, George; *The Butterfield Trail in New Mexico*; Yucca Enterprises; Las Cruces NM; 2005

Julyan, Robert; *The Place Names of New Mexico*; University of New Mexico Press; Albuquerque; 1998

Marcy, Randolph Barnes; *The Prairie Traveler - A Handbook for Overland Expeditions*; New York; Harper & Brothers; 1859; also accessible on internet at http://books.google.com/books?id=cWkoAAAAYAAJ&printsec=frontcover&dq=the+prairie+traveler&ei=7mjuS92iD4q4NaHf6cYP&cd=1#v=onepage&q&f=false

Matt, Don & Paul Matt; *The Great Butterfield Stage Expedition*; Internet publication; http://butterfieldoverlandmail.blogspot.com (accessed Jan 20, 2010).

Nienke, William & Sam Morrow; *Texas Historical Markers Database*; Internet publication (2005) at http://www.9key.com/markers/index.asp (accessed March 27, 2010)

Pike, Art; *New Mexico Wanderings*; Internet publication; (accessed Feb 18 2008 - not accessible March 17, 2010)

United States National Park Service; *El Camino Real de Tierra Adentro National Trail Comprehensive Management Plan*, published by U.S. Department of the Interior, National Park Service; Washington DC; 2004; also accessible via Internet at http://www.nps.gov/elca/parkmgmt/comprehensive-management-plan.htm

United States War Department, Topographical Engineers; *Map of Texas and Parts of New Mexico*; published by H.F. Walling, New York; 1857; Interactive Internet version at David Rumsey Map Collection; Internet accessible at http://www.davidrumsey.com/luna/servlet/detail/RUMSEY~8~1~4226~340 025:Map-of-Texas-and-part-of-New-Mexico (accessed November 29, 2010)

White, James W.; *History of Doña Ana County Post Offices;* published by the author; 1997. Selection internet accessible at http://www.rootsweb.ancestry.com/~nma/donaana/berino_cemetery.htm (accessed March 17, 2010)

Cottonwoods Ranch to Fort Fillmore

April 15, 2010

Cottonwoods Station - Berino, NM • Doña Ana County (N32° 4' 5.19", W106° 37' 15.08")

TO Fort Fillmore - north of Mesquite, NM • Doña Ana County (N32° 13' 25.72", W106° 43' 10.88")

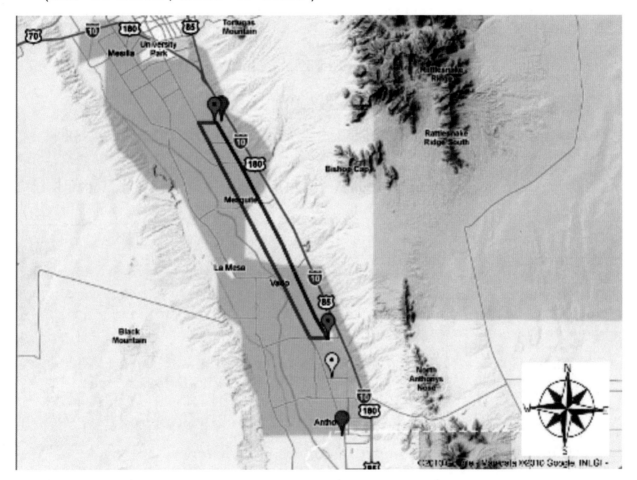

Approximate Actual Route, Cottonwoods Ranch to Fort Fillmore 17

miles from Anthony NM; 15 miles from Joy RD; 12 miles from Berino NM (1858 Bailey Itinerary says "25 miles" - possibly 15 miles?

Ormsby says 18 miles from Cottonwoods Ranch to Fort Fillmore)

Secondary Landmarks:

Cottonwoods Ranch per Hackler - N31° 59' 52", W106° 36' 30"

Cottonwoods Ranch (approximate) per Bailey mileage - Joy Road near NM Highway 478

Fort Fillmore per Hackler - N31° 59' 52", W106° 36' 30"

Notes:

The ongoing Butterfield Route into New Mexico continues to follow the Camino Real de Tierra Adentro trail, the 1849 Marcy Trail to Doña Ana and Bartlett's Texas-Mexico Boundary survey route. It is also quite clearly depicted on the 1857 War Department Topographical Engineers Map.

It is also clear the route followed the road established by Skillman, Wasson, Birch et al. for the San Antonio - San Diego Line. Here again, the route follows the elevated alluvial terrace above the flood plain between current state highway 478 and Interstate 10.

In modern terms, George Hackler and the Matt Brothers have investigated this segment.

Additional exploration of this route was done beginning in 1850 by John Russell Bartlett as U.S. Boundary Commissioner to establish the Mexico - U.S. border in accord with the Treaty of Guadalupe Hidalgo. While it can be argued whether Bartlett's attempts to settle the boundary location were successful, he did leave a record of his explorations and findings in an 1854 two-volume narrative of his expeditions.

The eventual settlement of the border took place after the Gadsden Purchase (December 1853) formally established the boundary between Mexico and the U.S. -- which fact, however had little impact on the actual Butterfield Route, which followed previously-established trail rights-of-way.

Ormsby and Bailey are at odds regarding the distance between Cottonwoods Station and Fort Fillmore. Ormsby notes the distance as 18 miles, while Bailey measures the distance at 25 miles.

According to military records, Fort Fillmore was established in 1851 by Col. E.V. Sumner, the commander of the New Mexico Territory Military Department, to protect the nearby settlement of Mesilla and the southern trail of the "Forty-niners" headed for California. Some maintain, however, that the post was established more as a social experiment to build an agriculturally self-sufficient military post far from the "earthly pleasures" tempting off-duty soldiers stationed at El Paso and the Mesilla Valley. It was one of several small military encampments served by the Butterfield. The fort was built out of adobe.

The camp at Fort Fillmore reportedly divided along ideological lines as Civil War became a reality, with some of the soldiers being Union sympathizers while others sided with the Confederacy.

The post was captured by Confederate Lt. Colonel John R. Baylor and a force of Texas cavalrymen on July 25, 1861. Baylor's Confederate troops were deployed back to Texas later that year. Thereafter, the fort lay abandoned and was recaptured by Union Forces. It was officially closed by the Union in October of 1862.

There is little left of Fort Fillmore, and even the site is difficult to locate. The majority of the site has been cultivated over and planted in pecan trees. It is located approximately 2.74 miles south southeast of the interchange of Interstate 10 and 25, and is approximately .2 miles west of Interstate 10. The site is privately owned. There are no surface indications that the fort ever existed.

Francis and Roberta Fugate, in their *Roadside History of New Mexico,* noted as of 1989 that "Today, not a trace of Fort Fillmore is visible. There is not even a historical marker to commemorate the ill-fated post."

According to the excellent article *Looking for Fort Fillmore* by researcher Jim Reed for the southernnewmexico.com (Burch Media / Clovis, NM):

> Johnson's New Military Map of the United States, a replica of a map printed for the United States War Department in the year 1861, places all the Forts, Military Posts, etc., and shows Fort Fillmore, Arizona Territory, positioned aside the Rio Grande, just above Fort Bliss, Texas and below Fort Thorn, Arizona. My modern-day *H.M. Gousha map of New Mexico* shows a Point of Interest symbol for the "Fort Fillmore Ruins" just below Las Cruces between State Road 478 and Interstate 10.

He then poignantly describes his quest for the elusive fort location. His conclusion notes thus:

> I still harbor hopes that something remains of Fort Fillmore. After about a mile, Fort Fillmore Road ends. There are 'No Trespassing' signs posted, metal gates and irrigation ditches, but no Fort Fillmore. In disbelief I look eastward towards the traffic on Interstate 10. No ruins visible.

My camera captures a large cottonwood, several groves of perfectly aligned pecan trees and the 'No Trespassing' sign, but no remnants of primitive adobe buildings, no historical marker. A man drives up to the mailbox post seeking his mail. His response to my Fort Fillmore query: 'It's all plowed up and turned to pecan groves.'

While Reed apparently got as close as one can get to the fort site, the good news is that someone apparently knows exactly where Fort Fillmore is. It is listed as "Address Restricted - Las Cruces" on the National Register of Historical Places (1974 - #74001196).

Reed's description places the Fort Fillmore site in the vicinity of coordinates N32° 13' 25.72", W106° 43' 10.88".

Hackler identifies the site of Fort Fillmore on private property slightly east of the listed endpoint location at coordinates N32° 13' 27", W106° 42' 48" -- approximately .2 mile east of the Reed location.

Greene mentions Fort Fillmore as being "wedged between I-10 and New Mexico Highway 478 about six miles south of Las Cruces" but does not further elucidate a location.

References:

Bailey, Goddard; *California -- Arrival of the Overland Mail -- Itinerary of the Route*; as reported by newspaper article; *New York Times* (NY) - October 14, 1858.

Bailey, Goddard; *Report to Postmaster A.V. Brown - Full itinerary as reported by De Bow's Review and Industrial Resources, Statistics etc;* published by De Bow's Review; New Orleans and Washington City; 1858. See specifically *Internal Improvements - 1. Wagon Road to the Pacific;* pp 719-721. Internet accessible at http://books.google.com/books?id=5CYoAAAAYAAJ&pg=PA720&lpg=PA720&dq=Cienega+de+los+Pimas&source=bl&ots=_5lZw_Bq23&sig=T6scCb8cpbY7KwjxpYoNvZpcgvI&hl=en&ei=i6KnS6KNOIr2M5yprIED&sa=X&oi=book_result&ct=result&resnum=2&ved=0CAwQ6AEwAQ#v=onepage&q=Cienega%20de%20los%20Pimas&f=false (accessed March 22, 2010).

Bartlett, John Russell; *Personal Narrative of Explorations and Incidents in Texas, New Mexico, California, Sonora and Chihuahua - Vol. One*; D. Appleton and Company; *New York; 1854*

Conkling, Roscoe P. and Margaret B.; *The Butterfield Overland Mail, 1857–1869* (3 vols.); Glendale, CA: A. H. Clark Company, 1947.

Fugate, Francis L. & Roberta B. Fugate; *Roadside History of New Mexico*; Mountain Press Publishing Company; Missoula MT; 1989.

Greene, A.C.; *900 Miles on the Butterfield Trail*; University of North Texas Press; 1994.

Hackler, George; *The Butterfield Trail in New Mexico*; Yucca Enterprises; Las Cruces NM; 2005.

Julyan, Robert; *The Place Names of New Mexico*; University of New Mexico Press; Albuquerque; 1998.

Marcy, Randolph Barnes; *The Prairie Traveler - a Handbook for Overland Expeditions*; New York; Harper & Brothers; 1859; also accessible on internet at http://books.google.com/books?id=cWkoAAAAYAAJ&printsec=frontcover&dq=the+prairie+traveler&ei=7mjuS92iD4q4NaHf6cYP&cd=1#v=onepage&q&f=false

Matt, Don & Paul Matt; *The Great Butterfield Stage Expedition*; Internet publication; http://butterfieldoverlandmail.blogspot.com (accessed Jan 20, 2010).

National Register of Historical Places; *New Mexico - Doña Ana County*; Internet publication at http://www.nationalregisterofhistoricplaces.com/NM/Dona+Ana/vacant.html (accessed 24 May 2010).

Reed, Jim; *Looking for Fort Fillmore*; Southern New Mexico Travel and Tourism; Burch Media; Clovis NM; Internet publication; http://www.southernnewmexico.com/Articles/Southwest/Dona_Ana/LookingforFortFillmore.html (accessed March 17, 2010).

United States National Park Service; *El Camino Real de Tierra Adentro National Trail Comprehensive Management Plan*, published by U.S. Department of the Interior, National Park Service; Washington DC; 2004; also accessible via Internet at http://www.nps.gov/elca/parkmgmt/comprehensive-management-plan.htm

United States War Department, Topographical Engineers; *Map of Texas and Parts of New Mexico*; published by H.F. Walling, New York; 1857; Interactive Internet version at David Rumsey Map Collection; Internet accessible at http://www.davidrumsey.com/luna/servlet/detail/RUMSEY~8~1~4226~340025:Map-of-Texas-and-part-of-New-Mexico (accessed November 29, 2010).

Fort Fillmore to Mesilla

January 05, 2011

Fort Fillmore - north of Mesquite, NM • Doña Ana County (N32° 13' 25.72", W106° 43' 10.88")

TO Mesilla Station ("La Posta") - Mesilla, NM • Doña Ana County (N32° 16' 27.84", W106° 47' 40.09")

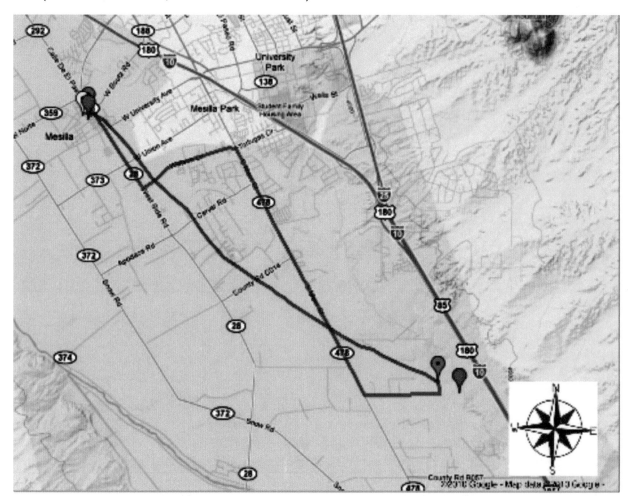

Approximate Actual Route, Fort Fillmore to Mesilla 5.75 miles

(No available comparable mileage per Bailey –

Ormsby says 6 miles from Fort Fillmore to Mesilla)

Secondary Landmarks:

Butterfield Administrative Offices per Fred Yeck and local reports – 113938 Calle Principal, Mesilla NM - N32° 16' 26.04", W106° 47' 42.72"

La Mesilla Station per Hackler - Calle Principal, Mesilla NM - N32° 16' 23", W106° 47' 40"

Notes:

Here again, the Butterfield Route continues to follow the Camino Real de Tierra Adentro Trail, known after Mexican Independence as Camino Nacional and the Chihuahua Trail, the 1849 Marcy Trail to Doña Ana and Bartlett's Texas-Mexico Boundary survey route of 1850-1853 as well as the San Antonio – San Diego Stagecoach route.

Marcy notes specifically that "From El Paso to Mesilla Valley in the Gadsden Purchase, the road runs up the east bank of the Rio Grande to Fort Fillmore (N.M.), where it crosses the river into the Mesilla Valley."

This route is also quite clearly depicted on the 1857 War Department Topographical Engineers Map, although it shows the road staying to the east of the Rio Grande from Fort Fillmore to Las Cruces (Mesilla) and on to Doña Ana.

Ormsby, however, specifically notes that "Between Fort Fillmore and Mesilla we forded the Rio Grande – at this point but an insignificant puddle, being very low. The water is very muddy and the shifting quicksands change the bed of the river much."

Ormsby's quote takes on particular relevance when comparing the early route maps to modern maps. Modern maps clearly place both Fort Fillmore and Mesilla's old town on the east bank of the Rio Grande. This fact would indicate that the modern river has shifted westward, obviating the need for a crossing between Fort Fillmore and Mesilla.

The route through this segment also continues to follow the road established by Skillman, Wasson, Birch et al. for the San Antonio - San Diego Line along the western foot of the Organ Mountains east of the Rio Grande.

In modern terms, George Hackler and the Matt Brothers have investigated this segment in some depth.

The next stop on the route, Mesilla, is at one of the very few actual Butterfield Station structures that remains intact.

34

It is now the location of La Posta Restaurant, a long-famous eatery among fans of the "Wild West." Information from the restaurant notes:

> Earliest records indicate the La Posta Compound was originally constructed in the 1840's. Sam Bean and his brother Roy Bean, operated a freight and passenger service line to Pinos Altos from this building in the 1850's. ... The La Posta Compound became an important stop on the Butterfield Stagecoach Line. During the 1870's and 1880's, the Corn Exchange Hotel, one of the finest lodges in the Southwest, operated from the building.

> John Davis, the proprietor of the hotel, died in the late 1870's, however, his wife Augustina continued to operate the hotel, a restaurant and other businesses in the building until the early 1900's. La Posta de Mesilla Restaurant originated in the northwest corner of the building in 1939 by Katy Griggs Camunez. ... After Katy passed away, the property and business was acquired by a great niece, Jerean Camunez Hutchinson and her husband Tom, a.k.a. "Hutch", who continue to offer the same quality food and great service in the unique dining environment Katy created.

There are also indications that the Overland Mail Company maintained separate administrative offices at Mesilla at a location near the La Posta Station.

Bartlett specifically mentions Mesilla in his pre-Butterfield route notes.

Bailey does not mention Mesilla in his itinerary and mileages. Ormsby notes the distance from Fort Fillmore to Mesilla as 6 miles and discusses the settlement at Mesilla specifically -- although he didn't seem to like it very much. Diplomatically stated, Ormsby's description of the town was "not complimentary."

As to the settlement of Mesilla itself, a local tourism website, www.oldmesilla.org, reports:

> "Mesilla is the best known and most visited historic community in southern New Mexico. Before it was bypassed by the railroad in 1881, it was the largest town between San Antonio and San Diego in the United States and a regional center for commerce and transportation. The traditional adobe buildings remain as a tangible reminder of its long and significant past.

After 1800, the vicinity of Mesilla was a camping and foraging spot for both the Spaniards and Mexicans. It wasn't until after the treaty of Guadalupe Hidalgo in 1848 that the first permanent settlers came to Mesilla to make it their home. By 1850, Mesilla was a firmly established colony.

The constant threat of attack by the Apache put these early settlers on constant alert. Apaches periodically swept through the Mesilla area, stealing livestock and foodstuffs, murdering colonists and seizing captives. Just as frequently the villages swiftly retaliated by sending out the Mesilla Guard, a militia comprised of a man from each household. Time after time the militia wrought revenge on any Apache in the area. In 1851, Apache depredations in the Valley caused the United States government to establish Fort Fillmore to protect the newly conquered territory and its people.

As a result of the Mexican War and the Treaty of Guadalupe Hidalgo, Mesilla was within the strip of land claimed by both the United States and Mexico, a "no man's land". In 1854, the village, being closer to the fort than either Las Cruces or Dona Ana, became the supply center for the garrisoned troops, providing entertainment, food, hay and building materials. The Mexican inhabitants of Mesilla also provided the knowledge needed to build a fort of adobe. The colony of Mesilla flourished. It was a major stop on the crossroads of the Chihuahua trail, and now the fort demanded items Easterners were accustomed to having. Business prospered and Anglo merchants such as Reynolds, Griggs and Bean, many of whom had come with the first armies were among those who reaped the profits of commerce. In 1854, The Gadsden Purchase determined Mesilla as officially part of the United States. As Mesilla was the most important community in this parcel, the treaty was consummated by the raising of the American flag on the town plaza with much ceremony on November 16, 1854.

The United States government now had a reliable route to the west coast and encouraged stage and freight services connecting California and the eastern states. The San Antonio-San Diego Mail began offering mail and passenger services 1857. The Butterfield Overland Mail and stage Line, established in 1858, set up its regional headquarters in Mesilla ... some of the finest hotels and restaurants in the region such as El Meson and the Texas-Pacific Hotel did booming business during this period. Within ten years of settlement, Mesilla had gone from a tiny colony struggling for survival to the largest and most important town in the area."

The Mesilla central plaza is listed on the National Register of Historic Places (Mesilla Plaza; 1966 - #66000475) and is also a National Historic Landmark. That documentation indicates the Butterfield administrative offices were located "at the El Patio Bar" as of 1966. This placement creates some confusion in that as of 2011, one location known as El Patio Bar is located at 2171 Calle de Parian (coordinates N32° 16' 25.39", W106° 47' 44.79"), three blocks southwest of La Posta. Another "El Patio Bar" is located at 113938 Calle Principal immediately southwest of the La Posta site.

Local sources report, however, that in 1966 the correct "El Patio Bar" was located immediately behind La Posta, facing on Calle Principal in the Mesilla Main Plaza. In corresponcence as of December 2011, Butterfield researcher Fred Yeck of Arizona reports coordinates for the El Patio on Calle Principal as N32° 16' 26.04", W106° 47' 42.72", which findings match perfectly to the local reports regarding the 1966 National Register data.

In view of these findings, the El Patio location at 2171 Calle de Parian (coordinates N32° 16' 25.39", W106° 47' 44.79") must be disregarded as a spurious site, with correct coordinates for the Butterfield Administrative Offices at N32° 16' 26.04", W106° 47' 42.72" on Calle Principal.

Hackler places the Mesilla station along Calle Principal in the same general vicinity at coordinates N32° 16' 23", W106° 47' 40" -- about one block south of the locally reported El Patio location and Yeck's coordinates.

The Matt Brothers visited La Posta Mesilla on their journey in 2004, noting "... the town, offered an amazing time warp back to the 1850's. The entire square seemed composed of original buildings in fantastic condition."

Greene also writes at some length about the Mesilla Station as do the Fugates and Julyan. Local historian Mary Daniels Taylor also includes a concise albeit brief chapter on the Butterfield in her book *A Place as Wild as the West Ever Was (Mesilla, New Mexico 1848 – 1872).*

References:

Bailey, Goddard; *California -- Arrival of the Overland Mail -- Itinerary of the Route*; as reported by newspaper article; *New York Times* (NY) - October 14, 1858.

Bailey, Goddard; *Report to Postmaster A.V. Brown - Full itinerary as reported by De Bow's Review and Industrial Resources, Statistics etc.;* published by *De Bow's Review*; New Orleans and Washington City; 1858. See specifically *Internal Improvements - 1. Wagon Road to the Pacific*; pp. 719-721. Internet

accessible at
http://books.google.com/books?id=5CYoAAAAYAAJ&pg=PA720&lpg=PA720&dq=Cienega+de+los+Pimas&source=bl&ots=_5lZw_Bq23&sig=T6scCb8cpbY7KwjxpYoNvZpcgvI&hl=en&ei=i6KnS6KNOIr2M5yprIED&sa=X&oi=book_result&ct=result&resnum=2&ved=0CAwQ6AEwAQ#v=onepage&q=Cienega%20de%20los%20Pimas&f=false (accessed March 22, 2010).

Bartlett, John Russell; *Personal Narrative of Explorations and Incidents in Texas, New Mexico, California, Sonora and Chihuahua - Vol. One*; D. Appleton and Company; New York; 1854.

Conkling, Roscoe P. and Margaret B.; *The Butterfield Overland Mail, 1857–1869* (3 vols.); Glendale, CA: A. H. Clark Company, 1947.

Fugate, Francis L. & Roberta B. Fugate; *Roadside History of New Mexico*; Mountain Press Publishing Company; Missoula MT; 1989.

Greene, A.C.; *900 Miles on the Butterfield Trail*; University of North Texas Press; 1994.

Hackler, George; *The Butterfield Trail in New Mexico*; Yucca Enterprises; Las Cruces NM; 2005.

Julyan, Robert; *The Place Names of New Mexico*; University of New Mexico Press; Albuquerque; 1998.

La Posta de Mesilla; *History*; informational brochure, published by proprietors of La Posta; internet publication at

http://www.laposta-de-mesilla.com/html/history.html.

Marcy, Randolph Barnes; *The Prairie Traveler - a Handbook for Overland Expeditions*; New York; Harper & Brothers; 1859; also accessible on internet at
http://books.google.com/books?id=cWkoAAAAYAAJ&printsec=frontcover&dq=the+prairie+traveler&ei=7mjuS92iD4q4NaHf6cYP&cd=1#v=onepage&q=Messilla&f=false

Matt, Don & Paul Matt; *The Great Butterfield Stage Expedition*; Internet publication; http://butterfieldoverlandmail.blogspot.com (accessed Jan 20, 2010).

National Register of Historic Places; *National Register Locations by State*; Internet publication; accessible at

http://www.nationalregisterofhistoricplaces.com/state.html (accessed May 3, 2010).

OldMesilla.org; *History of Mesilla*; Internet publication; accessible at

http://www.oldmesilla.org/html/history_of_mesilla.html (accessed May 27, 2010).

Ormsby, Waterman L.; *The Butterfield Overland Mail (Only Through Passenger on the First Westbound Stage)*; original publications *New York Herald* (NY) Sep 26 - Nov 19, 1858; republished by Henry E. Huntington Library and Art Gallery, San Marino CA, 1942 – 1998.

Taylor, Mary Daniels; *A Place as Wild as the West Ever Was (Mesilla, New Mexico 1848 – 1872)*; New Mexico State University; Las Cruces NM; 2004.

United States National Park Service; *El Camino Real de Tierra Adentro National Trail Comprehensive Management Plan*, published by U.S. Department of the Interior, National Park Service; Washington DC; 2004; also accessible via Internet at http://www.nps.gov/elca/parkmgmt/comprehensive-management-plan.htm.

United States War Department, Topographical Engineers; *Map of Texas and Parts of New Mexico*; published by H.F. Walling, New York; 1857; Interactive Internet version at David Rumsey Map Collection; Internet accessible at http://www.davidrumsey.com/luna/servlet/detail/RUMSEY~8~1~4226~340025:Map-of-Texas-and-part-of-New-Mexico (accessed November 29, 2010).

**La Posta de Mesilla Butterfield station site,
Mesilla NM (N32.2751, W106.7952).
Photo by Fred Yeck (2008).**

Mesilla to Picacho Pass

April 17, 2011

Mesilla Station ("La Posta") - Mesilla, NM • Doña Ana County (N32° 16' 27.84", W106° 47' 40.09")

TO Picacho Pass - Picacho, NM • Doña Ana County (N32° 20' 27.92", W106° 51' 22.43")

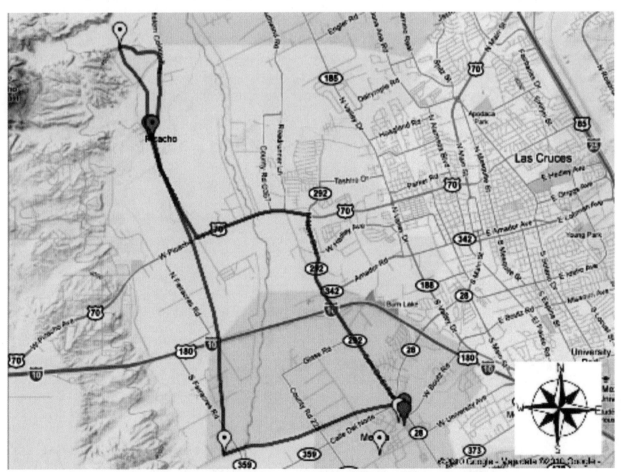

Approximate actual route Mesilla to Picacho Pass

7.75 miles - 13.75 miles from Fort Fillmore to Picacho Pass

(No exact comparable mileage. Bailey says 14 miles from Fort Fillmore to Picacho.)

Secondary Landmarks:

La Mesilla Historical Marker - (off route) Calle del Sur near Estrada Road, Mesilla NM - N32° 16' 1.00", W106° 47' 60.00"

Butterfield Trail Historical Marker - Mesilla Hills Drive near Bilbo Lane - approximate coordinates N32° 16' 0.00", W106° 49' 60.00"

Picacho Village - Picacho NM - N32° 19' 27.84", W106° 50' 57.70"

Picacho Station per Hackler - Picacho Village - N32° 16' 23", W106° 47' 40"

Notes:

The Butterfield Route from Mesilla to Picacho continues to follow the post-1849 routes mentioned by Marcy and Bartlett's Texas-Mexico Boundary survey route of 1850-1853. The route through this segment also continues to follow the road established by Skillman, Wasson, Birch et al. for the San Antonio - San Diego Line.

Marcy specifically mentions the route at Mesilla continuing via "Cook's" Spring to Tucson, but is rather vague about specifics. He does not specifically discuss the route from Mesilla to Picacho Pass, however.

The Butterfield Route appears to diverge from the Camino Real at Mesilla. The Camino Real de Tiedrra Aldentro Trail as identified by the National Park Service continues out of Mesilla on a northward track to Doña Ana and beyond. This route is also depicted on the 1857 War Department Topographical Engineers Map. The Butterfield Route, however, tracks toward the west from Mesilla before turning northward to Picacho.

In modern terms, George Hackler and the Matt Brothers have investigated the Picacho segment in some depth. Taylor's description of the Butterfield Route through Mesilla also appears to this westerly –to-northward turn. Additionally, there is an historical marker to the west of the Mesilla Station (Mesilla Hills Drive near Bilbo Lane) that appears to help locate the route.

While the route from the Mesilla Station to the vicinity of the Mesilla Hills marker marks a rare "90-degree turn" in the Butterfield route. The Mesilla Hills marker is in the vicinity of the modern Rio Grande bridge along Calle del Norte ("Road of the North). From that point northward, the old road followed a broad valley between the river to the east and mountains to the west toward the village of Picacho and its westward turn into Picacho Pass. Calle del Norte in particular were mentioned by Taylor and Hackler as being part of the Butterfield route.

There are two notable state historical markers located in Mesilla on the continuing route to Picacho Station / Picacho Pass. The first is located along Calle del Sur near Estrada Road (west of La Posta - approximate coordinates N32° 16' 1.00", W106° 47' 60.00"). This marker is slightly off of the actual Butterfield Route proper but gives us a good overview of the community history. That marker notes:

> "La Mesilla --After the Treaty of Guadalupe Hidalgo, which concluded the Mexican War in 1848, the Mexican government commissioned Cura Ramon Ortiz to settle Mesilla. He brought families from New Mexico and from Paso del Norte (modern Ciudad Juarez) to populate the Mesilla Civil Colony Grant, which by 1850 had more than 800 inhabitants.
>
> On November 16, 1854, a detachment from nearby Fort Fillmore raised the U.S. flag here confirming the Gadsden Purchase; thus, the Gadsden territory was officially recognized as part of the United States. In 1858, the Butterfield stage began its run through Mesilla. During the Civil War, Mesilla was the capital of the Confederate Arizona Territory."

The second marker is the ubiquitous Mesilla Hills Drive near Bilbo Lane location (approximate coordinates N32° 16' 0.00", W106° 49' 60.00").

That marker states "Butterfield Trail - Stagecoaches of the Butterfield Overland Mail Company began carrying passengers and mail from Saint Louis to San Francisco, across southern New Mexico, in 1858. The 2,795-mile journey took 21-22 days. In 1861 the service was rerouted through Salt Lake City. From La Mesilla west, the trail paralleled I-10."

By most reports, the actual Picacho Station was located just south of the Picacho Pass at Picacho Village (N32° 19' 27.84", W106° 50' 57.70"). While this segment report uses a terminus at Picacho Pass, it is important to note the actual Butterfield Station was located at Picacho Village.

Robert Julyan, in his 1998 revision of *Place Names of New Mexico,* notes that "this inhabited settlement once was a stop on the Butterfield Overland Mail Route."

According to New Mexico researcher Art Pike in his *New Mexico Wanderings*, "(Picacho Village) was settled in 1855 by Candelario Chavez together with people from Socorro, New Mexico. The original name for the settlement was Picacho de los Nevarez or "peak of the Nevarez family". Picacho Village once was a stop on the Butterfield Overland Mail route. Today (2002) the Church is at the center of the village, surrounded by homes, mobile homes and farms."

North of Picacho village is another important point along the route. The Butterfield route passed "through Box Canyon and Picacho Pass" as it progressed west. While it is no longer possible to safely traverse Picacho Pass, this more distant point (N32° 20' 27.92", W106° 51' 22.43") brings the road to a northeastward view of Box Canyon from the mouth of Picacho Pass westward.

Julyan notes specifically that "The Butterfield Overland Mail route passed just to the north of Picacho Mountain" via this pass.

Ormsby specifically mentions Picacho Pass, noting that "Our road lay through what is called the Pecatch [Picacho] Pass, and, as I walked through it, it seemed to me rather mountainous. It was about two miles long and had some very bad hills. In comparison with other passes and cañons on the route, it was not very bad, though quite bad enough and all uphill."

Hackler's data concurs with the placement of Picacho Village as the station site and the placement of Picacho Pass. The Fugates specifically note the route through this area. The Matt Brothers did not visit the Picacho Pass area.

References:

Bailey, Goddard; *California -- Arrival of the Overland Mail -- Itinerary of the Route*; as reported by newspaper article; New York Times (NY) - October 14, 1858

Bailey, Goddard; *Report to Postmaster A.V. Brown - Full itinerary as reported by De Bow's Review and Industrial Resources, Statistics etc;* published by De Bow's Review; New Orleans and Washington City; 1858. See specifically *Internal Improvements - 1. Wagon Road to the Pacific*; pp 719-721. Internet accessible at http://books.google.com/books?id=5CYoAAAAYAAJ&pg=PA720&lpg=PA720&dq=Cienega+de+los+Pimas&source=bl&ots=_5lZw_Bq23&sig=T6scCb8cpbY7KwjxpYoNvZpcgvI&hl=en&ei=i6KnS6KNOIr2M5yprIED&sa=X&oi=book_result&ct=result&resnum=2&ved=0CAwQ6AEwAQ#v=onepage&q=Cienega%20de%20los%20Pimas&f=false (accessed March 22, 2010)

Bartlett, John Russell; *Personal Narrative of Explorations and Incidents in Texas, New Mexico, California, Sonora and Chihuahua - Vol. One*; D. Appleton and Company; *New York; 1854*

Conkling, Roscoe P. and Margaret B.; *The Butterfield Overland Mail, 1857–1869* (3 vols); Glendale, CA: A. H. Clark Company, 1947.

Fugate, Francis L. & Roberta B. Fugate; *Roadside History of New Mexico*; Mountain Press Publishing Company; Missoula MT; 1989

Hackler, George; *The Butterfield Trail in New Mexico*; Yucca Enterprises; Las Cruces NM; 2005

Julyan, Robert; *The Place Names of New Mexico*; University of New Mexico Press; Albuquerque; 1998

Marcy, Randolph Barnes; *The Prairie Traveler - A Handbook for Overland Expeditions*; New York; Harper & Brothers; 1859; also accessible on internet at http://books.google.com/books?id=cWkoAAAAYAAJ&printsec=frontcover&dq=the+prairie+traveler&ei=7mjuS92iD4q4NaHf6cYP&cd=1#v=onepage&q=Messilla&f=false

Matt, Don & Paul Matt; *The Great Butterfield Stage Expedition*; Internet publication; http://butterfieldoverlandmail.blogspot.com (accessed Jan 20, 2010).

Ormsby, Waterman L.; *The Butterfield Overland Mail (Only Through Passenger on the First Westbound Stage)*; original publications New York Herald (NY) Sep 26 - Nov 19, 1858; republished by Henry E. Huntington Library and Art Gallery, San Marino CA, 1942 - 1998

Taylor, Mary Daniels; *A Place as Wild as the West Ever Was (Mesilla, New Mexico 1848 – 1872*; New Mexico State University; Las Cruces NM; 2004

United States National Park Service; *El Camino Real de Tierra Adentro National Trail Comprehensive Management Plan*, published by U.S. Department of the Interior, National Park Service; Washington DC; 2004; also accessible via Internet at http://www.nps.gov/elca/parkmgmt/comprehensive-management-plan.htm

United States War Department, Topographical Engineers; *Map of Texas and Parts of New Mexico*; published by H.F. Walling, New York; 1857; Interactive Internet version at David Rumsey Map Collection; Internet accessible at http://www.davidrumsey.com/luna/servlet/detail/RUMSEY~8~1~4226~340025:Map-of-Texas-and-part-of-New-Mexico (accessed November 29, 2010)

Picacho Pass to Cooke's Spring

April 19, 2011

Picacho / Box Canyon / Picacho Pass - Picacho, NM • Doña Ana County
(N32° 20' 27.92", W106° 51' 22.43")

**TO Cooke's Spring / Fort Cummings - north of Deming, NM •
Luna County** (N32° 27' 23.70", W107° 39' 33.55")

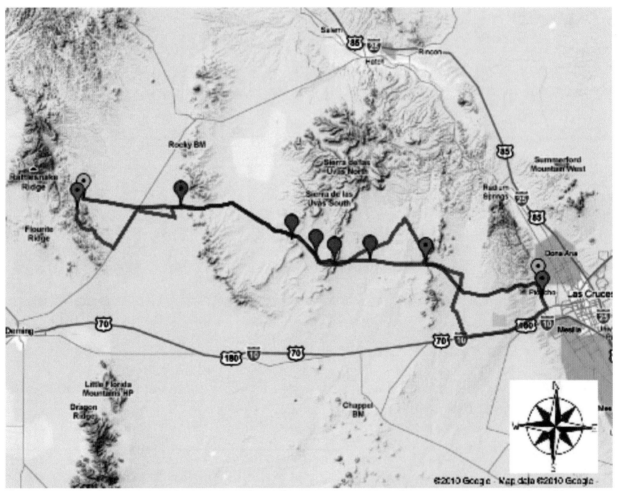

Approximate Actual Route Picacho Pass to Cooke's Spring 51.5 miles.

(1858 Bailey itinerary says 52 miles.)

Secondary Landmarks:

Picacho Peak - landmark - the mountain for which the nearby village and the adjacent pass were named - approximate coordinates N32° 20' 27.92", W106° 51' 22.43"

Rough and Ready Station per Hackler - approximate coordinates N32° 22'16", W107 03' 05"

Magdalena Gap per Hackler - landmark - approximate coordinates N32° 22' 24", W107 12' 30"

Massacre Peak per Hackler - landmark - approximate coordinates N32° 23' 02", W107 14' 24"

Massacre Gap per Hackler - landmark - approximate coordinates N32° 24' 20.00", W107° 17' 0.00"

Goodsight Station per Hackler - approximate coordinates N32° 26' 58", W107° 28' 39"

Cooke's Spring (actual) - per Chris Wray, Oregon-California Trails Association - approximate coordinates N32° 27' 46.34", W107° 38' 55"

Notes:

The route to Cooke's Spring remains arduous to this day. What Bailey gauged as a 52 mile trip (without water) in 1858 is now a 72 mile trip on existing roads via Interstate 10 and various back roads to far places -- although the original coach route amongst the mountains and valleys can be determined along a distance that approximates Bailey's mileage.

The actual route through this area continues to follow the post-1849 routes mentioned by Marcy and Bartlett's Texas-Mexico Boundary survey route of 1850-1853.

Cooke's Spring also represents a point at which the Marcy / Bartlett / Butterfield routes joined the Mormon Battalion Route to San Diego CA (1846 -1847).

Marcy specifically mentions the route continuing via "Cook's" (Cooke's) Spring to Tucson, but is rather vague about specifics. He does not specifically discuss the route from Picacho Pass to Cooke's Spring.

The route through this segment also continues to follow the road established by Skillman, Wasson, Birch et al. for the San Antonio - San Diego Line.

In modern terms, George Hackler has investigated this segment in some depth. The Matt Brothers' modern-road route did not include a visit to Cooke's Spring.

Mapping and field research teams of the Oregon - California Trails Association (OCTA) have also done a substantial amount of modern research on the Butterfield Route from Picacho Pass through the balance of New Mexico. While their data is not "published" per se, Chris Wray of OCTA has supplied the author with a substantial amount of mapping and locational data.

That data includes GPS readings of most of the important station sites and landmarks. It also includes GPS readings of locations where their researchers have discovered old wagon ruts, road scars and other evidence of early route usage. It also represents data derived from overlays of 1870s General Land Office maps on the Google Earth public GIS system.

That data, supplied on October 28, 2010, has also been taken into account in the preparation of this report and related map.

The OCTA data does not include the Picacho Station as such. The first marker within Picacho Pass as recorded by OCTA is at coordinates N32° 20' 21.47, W106° 52' 35.29"

The continuing route evidence readings clearly indicate Picacho Pass along the north foot of Picacho Peak and the route beyond that point to the west / northwest.

Hackler identifies a number of intermediate locations and landmarks that push the actual route From Picacho to Cooke's Spring through a mountainous passage well to the north of the modern I-10 corridor.

Of particular note amongst those are:

• Rough and Ready Station (approximate coordinates N32° 22'16", W107° 03' 05"). Of this station, Hackler notes that it was "established in December 1858 [and] was located in the gap between the Sleeping Lady Hills on the south and the Rough and Ready Hills on the north." Hackler also notes that the station was studied by archaeologist Joe Ben Sanders who "excavated the site and located and mapped the old Butterfield Station." He does not, however, state a date at which the Sanders study occurred. He also states that "The old wagon road is clearly visible today [2005] as it splits other ruins and passes on the south side of the station. This visibility is aided by the fact that the road was used long after the Butterfield era."

  The OCTA data clearly supports the mapped route data and places the Rough and Ready Station at the site as cited by Hackler.

• Magdalena Gap (approximate coordinates N32° 22' 24", W107° 12' 30"). Magdalena Gap, says Hackler, "... is a prominent feature on the Butterfield Trail between Rough and Ready and Goodsight [stations]." He adds that in this area, "... the Trail hits a three hundred foot rock wall. The only way through this wall is a crack called Magdalena Gap. The Butterfield Trail twisted through this rocky trap for two miles."

The OCTA data clearly supports the mapped route data and places Magdalena Gap approximately .7 miles east of the coordinates as cited by Hackler -- a nominal difference at worst.

• Massacre Peak (approximate coordinates N32° 23' 02", W107° 14' 24") and Massacre Gap (approximate coordinates N32° 24' 20.00", W107° 17' 0.00"). While the moniker "Massacre Peak" appears to post-date the Butterfield era, Hackler maintains that the trail predates the Butterfield as part of the San Antonio & San Diego Route and was used as a "joint route" by Butterfield and the SA&SD.

The OCTA data does not specifically label "Massacre Peak." It does, however, cite several evidentiary route markers (wagon ruts, road scar, etc.) to the north and northeast of the geological formation. This data is easily reconciled with Hackler's more specific citation and supports the mapped route.

• Goodsight Station (approximate coordinates N32° 26' 58", W107° 28' 39"). Hackler harks back to unpublished notes by Conkling regarding a station at Goodsight and readily cites the fact that no identifiable ruins have been discovered at this site. He does, however, cite field notes from Conkling that "Goodsight had at first the appearance of an Indian site because of its antiquity and proximity to the many old Indian ruins along the Mimbres, but the presence of many bent nails and old pieces of heavy china and other things found by the ranchmen make the site, without a doubt, not of Indian origin but the location of a station on the old trail." Hackler also cites a mention in the diaries of William Tallack (who traveled the Butterfield in 1860) noting that a fellow traveler joined the stage party at "Goodside" -- fourteen miles from Cooke's Spring. Hackler also notes that the water supply at Gooodsight was probably supplied by tank wagons from Cooke's Spring.

Hereagain, the OCTA data supports the mapped route with several intermediate evidentiary readings between Massacre Peak and Goodsight. The OCTA placement of the Goodsight Station notes the location at coordinates N32° 27' 0.35", W107° 26' 17.22" (approximately 2.3 miles east of Hackler's coordinates).

The evidence is compelling that the route from Picacho to Cooke's Spring followed the path described by Hackler and the OCTA utilizing the Mormon Battalion, San Antonio-San Diego and Marcy / Bartlett routes -- well to the north of the modern I-10 corridor but difficult to retrace along modern roads.

Cooke's Spring was named for Colonel Philip St. George Cooke who led the Mormon Battalion from Santa Fe, New Mexico, to California in 1846. The Mormon Battalion was a force drawn specifically from volunteers of the Mormon faith who accompanied and protected a group of fellow followers migrating from the area near Council Bluffs, Iowa, to new settlements in Utah.

Thereafter, the spring that Col. Cooke discovered remained an important trail stop in the New Mexico desert and was later protected by the establishment of Fort Cummings.

Fort Cummings was established at the Cooke's Spring site on October 2, 1863 under orders from Gen. James H. Carleton by Captain Valentine Dresher in command of Company B, 1st Infantry, California Volunteers. The fort was located approximately 53 miles west of the Rio Grande and 20 miles east of the Río Mimbres, the nearest watercourse west from the fort. The small post had adobe structures to accommodate one company. Fort Cummings was abandoned in 1873. It was then reopened in 1880 and finally closed permanently in November 1891.

There is a New Mexico Historical Marker at the fort location that reads "Fort Cummings -- This small and isolated post was built on the Mesilla - Tucson road to protect the Butterfield Trail against Apaches. Notorious Cooke's Canyon, located nearby, was a particularly dangerous point on the trail. Only ruins now remain of the 10-foot adobe walls that once surrounded [the small fort compound] ."

The coordinates for this marker location (N32° 27' 23.70", W107° 39' 33.55") represent the nearest point to Cooke's Spring / Fort Cummings by mapped road. In correspondence as of October 28, 2010, Chris Wray of the Oregon - California Trails Association (OCTA) stated that the actual spring and fort location according to their field studies is off-road about 4000 feet due northeast of this location (coordinates N32 27' 46.34", W107 38' 55").

Bailey specifically mentions the Cooke's Spring Station as does Ormsby.

Bartlett also specifies Cooke's Spring along the route through this area.

The Fugates and Julyan specifically identify Cooke's Spring as a Butterfield station site and as the later site for Fort Cummings.

References:

Bailey, Goddard; *California -- Arrival of the Overland Mail -- Itinerary of the Route*; as reported by newspaper article; New York Times (NY) - October 14, 1858

Bailey, Goddard; *Report to Postmaster A.V. Brown - Full itinerary as reported by De Bow's Review and Industrial Resources, Statistics etc.;* published by De Bow's Review; New Orleans and Washington City; 1858. See specifically *Internal Improvements - 1. Wagon Road to the Pacific*; pp 719-721. Internet accessible at http://books.google.com/books?id=5CYoAAAAYAAJ&pg=PA720&lpg=PA720& dq=Cienega+de+los+Pimas&source=bl&ots=_5lZw_Bq23&sig=T6scCb8cpbY7K wjxpYoNvZpcgvI&hl=en&ei=i6KnS6KNOIr2M5yprIED&sa=X&oi=book_result& ct=result&resnum=2&ved=0CAwQ6AEwAQ#v=onepage&q=Cienega%20de%20 los%20Pimas&f=false (accessed March 22, 2010)

Bartlett, John Russell; *Personal Narrative of Explorations and Incidents in Texas, New Mexico, California, Sonora and Chihuahua - Vol. One*; D. Appleton and Company; *New York; 1854*

Conkling, Roscoe P. and Margaret B.; *The Butterfield Overland Mail, 1857–1869* (3 vols); Glendale, CA: A. H. Clark Company, 1947.

Fugate, Francis L. & Roberta B. Fugate; *Roadside History of New Mexico*; Mountain Press Publishing Company; Missoula MT; 1989

Hackler, George; *The Butterfield Trail in New Mexico*; Yucca Enterprises; Las Cruces NM; 2005

Julyan, Robert; *The Place Names of New Mexico*; University of New Mexico Press; Albuquerque; 1998

Marcy, Randolph Barnes; *The Prairie Traveler - A Handbook for Overland Expeditions*; New York; Harper & Brothers; 1859; also accessible on internet at http://books.google.com/books?id=cWkoAAAAYAAJ&printsec=frontcover&dq =the+prairie+traveler&ei=7mjuS92iD4q4NaHf6cYP&cd=1#v=onepage&q=Mess illa&f=false

Oregon - California Trails Association; *Learn. Connect. Preserve.*; Internet publication accessible at http://www.octa-trails.org/ (accessed October 9, 2010)

Ormsby, Waterman L.; *The Butterfield Overland Mail (Only \Through Passenger on the First Westbound Stage)*; original publications New York Herald (NY) Sep 26 - Nov 19, 1858; republished by Henry E. Huntington Library and Art Gallery, San Marino CA, 1942 - 1998

**Butterfield Station ruins at Cooke's Spring
(N32.4656, W107.6464).
Photo by Fred Yeck (2008).**

Cooke's Spring to Cow Spring

April 19, 2011

Cooke's Spring / Fort Cummings - north of Deming, NM • Luna County
(N32° 27' 23.70", W107° 39' 33.55")

TO Cow Spring (Ojo de la Vaca) - near Old Town, NM • Luna County
(N32° 24 42.00", W108° 10' 42.00")

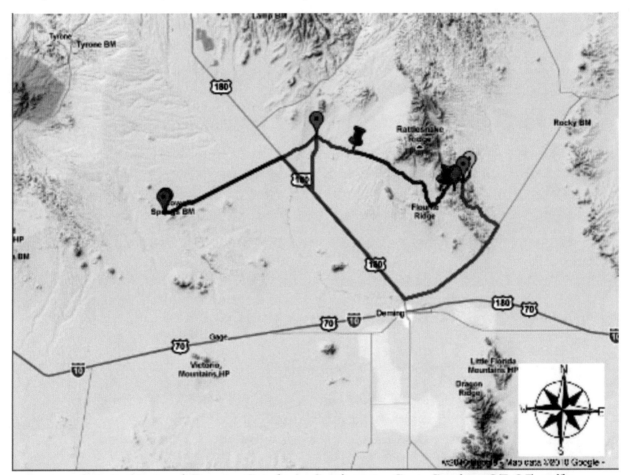

Approximate Actual Route Cooke's Spring to Cow Spring 37.25 miles - Cooke's to Miembres 20 miles; Miembres to Cow Spring 17.25 miles.

(1858 Bailey itinerary says 18 miles Cooke's Spring to Miembres River + 16 further to Cow Spring = 34 miles.)

Secondary Landmarks:

Cooke's Spring (actual) - per Chris Wray, Oregon - California Trails Association - approximate coordinates N32° 27' 46.34", W107° 38' 55"

Massacre Peak II per Hackler - approximate coordinates N32° 26' 39", W107° 40' 28"

"Orphaned" segment identified as Butterfield Trail on current maps - begin coordinates N32 26' 34.84", W107 41' 31.20" / end coordinates N32° 29' 56.61", W107° 50' 46.15"

Cow Spring Draw - south end - I-10 northwest of Deming - approximate coordinates N32° 13' 36.01", W108° 0' 54.00"

Ojo de Vaca (Cow Spring) per Wray / OCTA - coordinates N32° 24' 34.87", W108° 10' 53.40"

Notes:

There are some additional complications in the following two station locations along the actual route. Some researchers identify a "Murphy's Station" between Cooke's Spring and Cow Springs. Other researchers identify "Miembres Station" along the Miembres River.

No documentary trace has been found for "Murphy's Station" between Cooke's Spring and Cow Springs. It is possible that the name "Murphy's" refers to the "Miembres" location and is likely that the Indian word "Miembres" has been mistranslated by some as the recognizable Irish / Anglo-Saxon name "Murphy's".

Ormsby refers to crossing the "Membrace" river in this area while Bailey refers to a station with the name "Miembres".

The original Butterfield route from Cooke's Spring to Miembres and beyond to Cow Spring (by its Spanish name "Ojo de Vaca") can be identified on the post-1849 routes discussed by Marcy and Bartlett's Texas-Mexico Boundary survey route of 1850 - 1853.

Marcy specifically mentions the route continuing via "Rio Mimbres" and "Ojo de Vaca", but is rather vague about specifics.

Mentions of Rio Mimbres and Ojo de Vaca locations can also be found in several historical recollections of the Mormon Battalion Route of 1846-1847.

The route through this segment also continues to follow the road established by Skillman, Wasson, Birch et al. for the San Antonio - San Diego Line.

In modern terms, George Hackler has investigated this segment in some depth. The Matt Brothers followed a modern-road route through this segment bypassing Miembres and Cow Springs.

The Oregon - California Trails Association has done a significant amount of field research and mapping in this area. That data, supplied by Chris Wray of OCTA as of October 28, 2010, has also been taken into account in the preparation of this report and related map.

Mapping data supplied by Wray / OCTA also confirms the mapped route in detail.

The original Butterfield Route is no longer accessible immediately west of Cooke's Spring and again immediately east of Miembres, leaving an intervening stretch identified on modern maps as "Butterfield Trail" that is orphaned from modern roads.

On this leg, Hackler notes a secondary "Massacre Peak II" landmark on the route to Miembres. He cites that location at approximate coordinates N32° 26' 39", W107° 40' 28".

Not to be confused with the earlier citation, this "Massacre Peak" apparently was locally designated as the location of a different conflict between settlers and the Indian natives that is unrelated to the previously identified "Massacre Peak."

The Wray / OCTA data does not specify "Massacre Peak" as such but does follow the route as indicated by Hackler.

This "Massacre Peak" location helps to locate the original route immediately west of Cooke's Spring. It represents an intermediary point on the eastern end of the Butterfield Route between Cooke's Spring and the orphaned segment of the identified Butterfield Trail.

Hackler places the Miembres Station to the north and west of Deming in the vicinity of the community of Old Town (formerly "Mowry City") at approximate coordinates N32° 31' 20", W107° 54' 58". The Wray / OCTA data confirms this location with notations that it also compares to the route and station as identified in a map overlay using GLO maps of the area from the 1870s.

Julyan's *Place Names of New Mexico* notes of Miembres / Mowry City that "This locality began as a stop on the San Antonio & San Diego stage line.

About 1857, retired U.S. Army Lieutenant Sylvester Mowry, who was active in the territorial affairs of present-day Arizona, saw potential in the site and eventually went on to promote it as Mowry City. In 1858,the site became a stop on the Butterfield Overland Mail Route, but neither the stage line nor Mowry City lasted long, though the locality had a brief existence as 'Camp Miembres'."

Julyan also cites the location of "Mowry City / Camp Miembres" as "25 miles N of Deming" in the vicinity of Old Town NM and Dwyer NM -- which location would appear to concur with Hackler.

Continuing westward, modern roads do not follow the southwestward trajectory of the old route – meaning that automobile traffic must double-back along the modern auto route from Miembres to get to Cow Spring. On modern roads, it takes 23 miles to cover the 16-mile original route.

As to "Cow Spring", Bartlett specifically mentions following the 1846 - 1847 Mormon Battalion route pioneered by Cooke to "Ojo de Vaca" (Cow Spring).

Ormsby's 1858 account indicates that there were no permanent structures at the Cow Springs site, merely "... one tent for the accommodation of the station men ..." but does not specifically place the station or describe the route.

Bailey specifically mentions "Ojo de Vaca" as 16 miles from Miembres.

Julyan cites a stage station location as "Ojo de las Vacas" (Spring of the Cows) in Luna County, "west of the Miembres River".

By background, Julyan adds "According to George Adlai Feather [New Mexico scholar], this was a stop on the Butterfield Overland Mail Route that earlier had been a watering stop on the road from Santa Rita to Janos in Mexico. Metcalf, an 1849 American traveler, said the spring was named for cows that watered here. Feather said a hotel, probably small, operated here."

Julyan does not specifically locate the spring or station, however.

The Fugates specifically mention "Ojo de la Vaca" as a Butterfield Station site.

Hackler places the Cow Spring station at approximate coordinates N32° 24' 42", W108° 10' 42" but indicates that no ruins were located at the site.

The Wray / OCTA data notes this site as "Ojo de Vaca" and places it 0.3 miles southwest of the Hackler locations at coordinates N32° 24' 34.87", W108° 10' 53.40".

References:

Bailey, Goddard; *California -- Arrival of the Overland Mail -- Itinerary of the Route*; as reported by newspaper article; New York Times (NY) - October 14, 1858

Bailey, Goddard; *Report to Postmaster A.V. Brown - Full itinerary as reported by De Bow's Review and Industrial Resources, Statistics etc;* published by De Bow's Review; New Orleans and Washington City; 1858. See specifically *Internal Improvements - 1. Wagon Road to the Pacific*; pp 719-721. Internet accessible at http://books.google.com/books?id=5CYoAAAAYAAJ&pg=PA720&lpg=PA720&dq=Cienega+de+los+Pimas&source=bl&ots=_5lZw_Bq23&sig=T6scCb8cpbY7KwjxpYoNvZpcgvI&hl=en&ei=i6KnS6KNOIr2M5yprIED&sa=X&oi=book_result&ct=result&resnum=2&ved=0CAwQ6AEwAQ#v=onepage&q=Cienega%20de%20los%20Pimas&f=false (accessed March 22, 2010)

Bartlett, John Russell; *Personal Narrative of Explorations and Incidents in Texas, New Mexico, California, Sonora and Chihuahua - Vol. One*; D. Appleton and Company; *New York; 1854*

Conkling, Roscoe P. and Margaret B.; *The Butterfield Overland Mail, 1857–1869* (3 vols); Glendale, CA: A. H. Clark Company, 1947.

Fugate, Francis L. & Roberta B. Fugate; *Roadside History of New Mexico*; Mountain Press Publishing Company; Missoula MT; 1989

Hackler, George; *The Butterfield Trail in New Mexico*; Yucca Enterprises; Las Cruces NM; 2005

Julyan, Robert; *The Place Names of New Mexico*; University of New Mexico Press; Albuquerque; 1998

Marcy, Randolph Barnes; *The Prairie Traveler - A Handbook for Overland Expeditions*; New York; Harper & Brothers; 1859; also accessible on internet at http://books.google.com/books?id=cWkoAAAAYAAJ&printsec=frontcover&dq=the+prairie+traveler&ei=7mjuS92iD4q4NaHf6cYP&cd=1#v=onepage&q=Messilla&f=false

Oregon - California Trails Association; *Learn. Connect. Preserve.*; Internet publication accessible at http://www.octa-trails.org/ (accessed October 9, 2010)

Ormsby, Waterman L.; *The Butterfield Overland Mail (Only Through Passenger on the First Westbound Stage)*; original publications New York Herald (NY) Sep 26 - Nov 19, 1858; republished by Henry E. Huntington Library and Art Gallery, San Marino CA, 1942 – 1998

**Vicinity of Mimbres Station (N32.503, W107.924).
Photo by Fred Yeck (2008).**

Cow Spring to Soldiers' Farewell Hill

April 19, 2011

Cow Spring (Ojo de la Vaca) - near Old Town, NM • Luna County (N32° 24' 42.00", W108° 10' 42.00")

TO Soldiers' Farewell - east of Lordsburg, NM • Grant County (N32° 21' 23", W108° 22' 16.00"

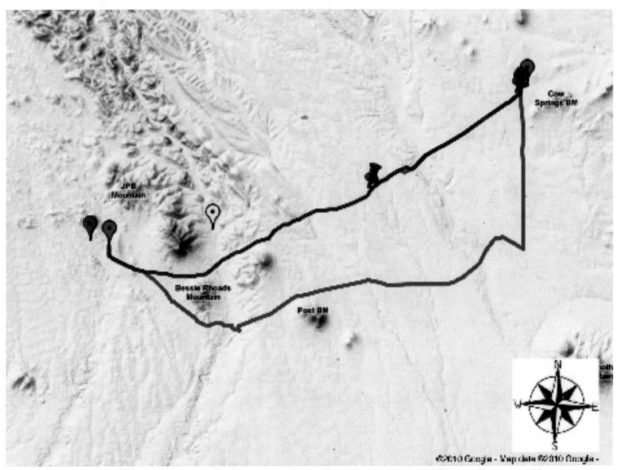

Approximate Actual Route Cow Spring to Soldiers Farewell

12.5 miles.

(1858 Bailey itinerary says 14 miles.)

Secondary Landmarks:

Ojo de Vaca (Cow Spring) per Wray / OCTA - coordinates N32° 24' 34.87", W108° 10' 53.40"

"Orphaned" segment identified as Butterfield Trail on current maps - begin coordinates N32° 24' 34.82", W108° 10' 53.99" / end coordinates N32° 22' 31.98", W108° 14' 47.32"

Soldiers' Farewell Hill (east foot) - south end - north west of Deming - approximate coordinates N32° 21' 24.12", W108° 19' 48.36"

Soldiers Farewell per Wray / OCTA - coordinates Longitude: - N32° 21' 25.19", W108° 22' 09.39"

Notes:

The Butterfield Route from Cow Spring to the next station at Soldiers Farewell is readily identifiable.

This segment follows the Mormon Battalion Route of 1846 - 1847. Marcy and Bartlett (1849 – 1853) appear to have bypassed Soldiers Farewell on their journeys, continuing southward instead into Mexico.

This segment continues along the San Antonio - San Diego Route established by Skillman, Wasson, Birch et al. (1857).

In modern terms, George Hackler has investigated this segment in depth. The Matt Brothers do not mention Soldiers Farewell.

The Oregon - California Trails Association has done a significant amount of field research and mapping in this area. That data, supplied by Chris Wray of OCTA on October 28, 2010, has also been taken into account in the preparation of this report and related map. Mapping data supplied by Wray / OCTA also confirms the mapped route in detail.

In context to the route through this area and as noted before, there is a 0.3 mile discrepancy between Hackler's placement for Cow Spring / Ojo de Vaca (coordinates N32° 24' 42.00", W108° 10' 42.00") and the Wray / OCTA placement slightly southwest (coordinates N32° 24' 34.87", W108° 10' 53.40"). That 0.3 mile proves relevant to following the actual Butterfield Route.

The modern track toward the west from Cow Spring intersects with a southwestward segment identified on some modern maps as "Butterfield Trail". On the eastern end, that "orphaned segment" begins at coordinates

N32° 24' 34.82", W108° 10' 53.99" -- which matches almost exactly to the Wray / OCTA location for Cow Spring at coordinates N32° 21' 25.19", W108° 22' 09.39".

This "orphaned segment" can be followed toward the southwest for approximately 5 miles to coordinates at N32° 22' 31.98", W108° 14' 47.32" where it terminates.

From that dead end, it is easy to visualize a terrain-based track continuing toward the southwest to Soldier's Farewell Hill. At that point, the route skirts the southern foot of the hill before cutting slightly north to the Butterfield Station site slightly east of Soldiers' Farewell Hill proper.

This track closely meshes with Bailey's measured mileage between the two stations to within a 1.5 mile tolerance for error.

In modern terms, George Hackler has investigated this segment in depth. The Matt Brothers did not investigate this route segment.

The Wray / OCTA field research and mapping data also reinforces the mapped route.

The next station along the Butterfield Route has one of the most "poetic" names to be found along the route. It is located at "Soldiers' Farewell Hill." This comparatively small hill in the New Mexico desert is far less imposing than its relative importance during the Butterfield period and the Civil War era.

Perhaps the poetry and the importance are best described in a *New York Times* article dated June 17, 1879 and titled "New Mexico's Prospects - Copper Enough For All The World". The article states, "Peculiar as the name may appear to the great outside world, it nevertheless had deep and significant meaning to the pioneers of 1860-1865. To the left, the Chiricahua Mountains loom up, dark and frowning and still the haunt of the treacherous Apache. But there are now hardly five where 10 to 15 years ago there were 100. In the Chiricahuas, the Pyramids and the Peloncillo were the Indian strongholds and woe to the luckless small party of hardy explorers which in the years past attempted passage through the canyons and other natural gateways. To this point, escorts detached from Army camps in the Territory accompanied all traveling parties not of themselves sufficient strength numerically to withstand attack, and here the troops bade them goodbye, hence the name given this point -- Soldiers' Farewell."

The 1879 article also notes, "There is little to note the spot -- an adobe house long since abandoned, a ranch of limited extent, and a spring. The latter by far the greatest of the attractions, for in this country the presence of water remaining wet the year 'round is indeed of greatest moment."

Julyan reports "At least three legends -- all from the late 1800s and all apocryphal -- explain this romantic name. One is that soldiers manning a signal station here -- mirrors by day, flares at night -- were trapped by Apaches and, tormented by thirst, signaled a farewell saying they were all going down to battle the Indians; all were killed. Another story says a soldier from the East, despondent over separation from his sweetheart, killed himself here. The most widely accepted story says soldiers, escorting wagon trains and travelers en route to California, were ordered to go no farther than here, where they were forced to say 'farewell.'"

The nearby promontory for which the station was named (approximate coordinates N32° 21' 24.12", W108° 19' 48.36") is located slightly west of the Butterfield station site as identified by Hackler.

Historically, it was also referred to as "Soldiers' Farewell" by Daniel Tyler, a member of the Mormon Battalion, as early as 1847. Bailey and Ormsby both speak directly of Soldiers' Farewell.

The Fugates specifically mention Soldiers' Farewell as a Butterfield site. Greene mentions the site -- noting that he was unable to locate it. The Matt Brothers also mention Soldiers' Farewell but did not visit the location.

Of the station site proper, Hackler notes that "The remains of a forty-foot by seventy-foot rock wall enclosure are still visible today [2005]. The walls were two feet thick at the base and ten feet high. The unmortared wall rocks are held in place by their weight and the interlocking pattern whereby a rock lays on at least two other rocks." He places the site at coordinates N32° 21' 23", W108° 22' 16.00".

The Wray / OCTA data places the specific Soldiers Farewell Station ruins at coordinates N32° 21' 25.19", W108° 22' 09.39" -- off of the public road approximately 2629.5 feet northwest of the coordinates as reported by Hackler.

References:

Bailey, Goddard; *California -- Arrival of the Overland Mail -- Itinerary of the Route*; as reported by newspaper article; New York Times (NY) - October 14, 1858

Bailey, Goddard; *Report to Postmaster A.V. Brown - Full itinerary as reported by De Bow's Review and Industrial Resources, Statistics etc*; published by De

Bow's Review; New Orleans and Washington City; 1858. See specifically *Internal Improvements - 1. Wagon Road to the Pacific*; pp 719-721. Internet accessible at http://books.google.com/books?id=5CYoAAAAYAAJ&pg=PA720&lpg=PA720& dq=Cienega+de+los+Pimas&source=bl&ots=_5lZw_Bq23&sig=T6scCb8cpbY7K wjxpYoNvZpcgvI&hl=en&ei=i6KnS6KNOIr2M5yprIED&sa=X&oi=book_result& ct=result&resnum=2&ved=0CAwQ6AEwAQ#v=onepage&q=Cienega%20de%20 los%20Pimas&f=false (accessed March 22, 2010)

Bartlett, John Russell; *Personal Narrative of Explorations and Incidents in Texas, New Mexico, California, Sonora and Chihuahua - Vol. One*; D. Appleton and Company; *New York; 1854*

Conkling, Roscoe P. and Margaret B.; *The Butterfield Overland Mail, 1857–1869* (3 vols); Glendale, CA: A. H.Clark Company, 1947.

Fugate, Francis L. & Roberta B. Fugate; *Roadside History of New Mexico*; Mountain Press Publishing Company; Missoula MT; 1989

Greene, A.C.; *900 Miles On the Butterfield Trail*; University of North Texas Press; 1994

Hackler, George; *The Butterfield Trail in New Mexico*; Yucca Enterprises; Las Cruces NM; 2005

Julyan, Robert; *The Place Names of New Mexico*; University of New Mexico Press; Albuquerque; 1998

Marcy, Randolph Barnes; *The Prairie Traveler - A Handbook for Overland Expeditions*; New York; Harper & Brothers; 1859; also accessible on internet at http://books.google.com/books?id=cWkoAAAAYAAJ&printsec=frontcover&dq =the+prairie+traveler&ei=7mjuS92iD4q4NaHf6cYP&cd=1#v=onepage&q=Mess illa&f=false

Matt, Don & Paul Matt; *The Great Butterfield Stage Expedition*; Internet publication http://butterfieldoverlandmail.blogspot.com (accessed Jan 20, 2010).

New York Times; New Mexico's Prospects - Copper Enough For All The World; June 17, 1879; internet accessible at http://query.nytimes.com/gst/abstract.html?res=9B07E3DA1E3FE63BBC4 F52DFB0668382669FDE (accessed March 19, 2010)

Oregon - California Trails Association; *Learn. Connect. Preserve*; Internet publication accessible at http://www.octa-trails.org/ (accessed October 9, 2010)

Ormsby, Waterman L.; *The Butterfield Overland Mail (Only Through Passenger on the First Westbound Stage)*; original publications New York Herald (NY) Sep 26 - Nov 19, 1858; republished by Henry E. Huntington Library and Art Gallery, San Marino CA, 1942 - 1998

**Vicinity of Soldiers' Farewell site
(N32.3568,W108.3692).
Photo by Fred Yeck (2008).**

Soldiers' Farewell Hill to Mexican Springs / Shakespeare

April 19, 2011

Soldiers' Farewell - east of Lordsburg, NM • Grant County (N32° 21' 23", W108° 22' 16")

TO Mexican Springs / Shakespeare, NM - southwest of Lordsburg, NM • Hidalgo County (N32° 19' 29.05", W108° 44' 17.93")

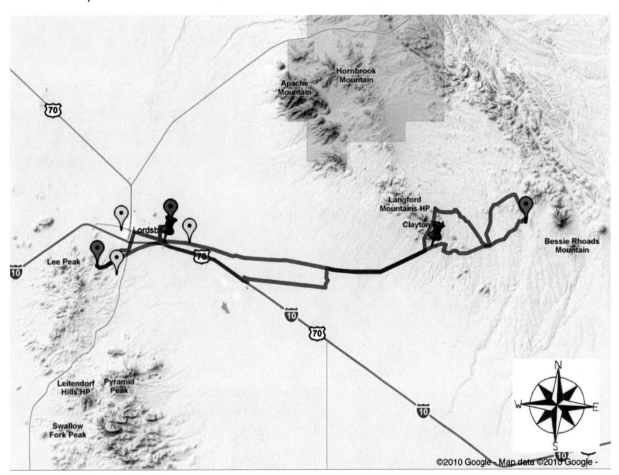

Approximate actual route Soldiers' Farewell to Shakespeare / Mexican Springs 25.25 miles.

(No exact comparable. 1858 Bailey itinerary says 42 miles to Steins.)

Secondary Landmarks:

"Orphaned segment" identified as Butterfield Trail on current maps - begin coordinates N32° 20' 16.30", W108° 26' 28.39" / end coordinates N32° 20' 31.58", W108° 40' 33.89"

Barney's Station (Lordsburg NM) per Matts - approximate coordinates N32° 20' 26.70", W108° 39' 27.90"

Barney's Station (Lordsburg NM) per Hackler - N32° 21' 16", W108° 40' 26"

Lordsburg Historical Marker - Short Park off of W 2nd Street near W Railway Boulevard, Lordsburg NM - approximate coordinates N32° 20' 60.00", W108° 43' 1.00"

Mexican Springs (near Shakespeare NM) per Hackler - approximate coordinates N32° 19' 03", W108° 43' 18"

Notes:

Some researchers have placed the next station location **at** Lordsburg; however, the actual location (or locations) used by Butterfield in this area remain open to discussion. The town of Lordsburg proper was not established until 1880.

As to the general route through this segment, it continues to track the due westward course followed by the Mormon Battalion route of 1846 - 1847 and the San Antonio - San Diego Stage route established by Skillman, Wasson, Birch et al. (1857).

In this area, many modern maps indicate an orphaned 14 mile segment of identified "Butterfield Trail" stretching from about the midpoint of the route into what is now Lordsburg (begin coordinates N32° 20' 16.30", W108° 26' 28.39" / end coordinates N32° 20' 31.58", W108° 40' 33.89").

In modern terms, George Hackler has done substantial study on this segment. The Matt Brothers indicated a visit to the station sites in this area but did not specifically investigate the old route.

Here again, the Oregon - California Trails Association has also done a significant amount of field research and mapping in this area. That data, supplied by Chris Wray of OCTA on October 28, 2010, has also been taken into account in the preparation of this report and related map.

Detailed input from Hackler and the mapping data supplied by Wray / OCTA confirms the mapped route in detail -- with minor deviations as will be noted below.

From the evidence, it is possible that several locations in the area of Lordsburg may have served as station sites during the Butterfield period. On the first runs in September - October of 1858, however, neither Ormsby nor Bailey mentions a stop in the vicinity of what is now Lordsburg. Bailey indicates an eastward segment of 42 miles (without water) between Soldiers' Farewell and the next station at Steins Peak. Ormsby reports the westward segment between Soldiers' Farewell and Steins -- noted likewise as "42 miles without water".

It is likely that John Butterfield would have established later intermediate stations to break the difficult trip through this area, and the vicinity of what would later become Lordsburg is a likely candidate for such locations.

Hackler notes that several mid- to late-1800s stage stations have been identified in the Lordsburg area and indicates that a location known as "Barney's Station" may be the most accurate identification of the Butterfield Station as of 1859. There is also a second, less-likely "contender" for Butterfield status at what is now the ghost town of Shakespeare in the vicinity of what was earlier known as Mexican Springs.

Hackler places the "Barney's Station" location to the northeast of Lordsburg proper (approximate coordinates N32 21' 16", W108 40' 26"). He notes specifically that "The location of Barney's is uncertain," but cites historical descriptions of the station as "a two-room adobe with water well."

The Matt Brothers place the Barney's Station site slightly southeast of Hackler's coordinates along the "orphaned segment" at approximate coordinates N32° 20' 26.70", W108° 39' 27.90" but do not mention Shakespeare / Mexican Springs.

It is important to note that both of these locations are in the immediate vicinity of the western end of the "orphaned" Butterfield Trail segment (coordinates N32° 20' 31.58", W108° 40' 33.89").

In correspondence as of October 28, 2010, Chris Wray of the Oregon - California Trails Association (OCTA) noted that the association's field research questions Hackler's placement for Barney's Station. He states that Hackler's location "... to the north is unlikely since it so far off the known road scar." OCTA data supports the closer accuracy of the Matt Brothers' measurement.

It should be noted, however, that comparing the end of the "Butterfield Trail Road Scar" at coordinates N32° 20' 31.58", W108° 40' 33.89" to the Matt Brothers' measurement at coordinates N32° 19' 29.05", W108° 44' 17.93" and Hackler's measurement at coordinates N32 21' 16", W108 40' 26" is a nominal difference. All three are easily within one mile of one another.

The Wray / OCTA mapping data also specifically notes the Hackler coordinates as a "possible" location for Barney's Station.

The Fugates make mention of "Barney's Stand" in the Lordsburg area but do not specify a location.

Greene does not speak directly to "Barney's Station," but does speak of a bitter financial and legal fight over the future of the Overland Mail as of 1861 between John Butterfield and one Danford N. Barney. Greene reports that Barney was a director of the Wells Fargo Company and of the Overland Mail Company who threatened foreclosure of debts against the Overland Mail Company if John Butterfield was not replaced as President. Greene reports that John Butterfield resigned "in protest" shortly thereafter. Whereupon Danford N. Barney dropped his foreclosure actions.

Julyan does not mention Barney's Station but does specifically identify Shakespeare with Mexican Springs and the Butterfield route.

It is also important to note that a New Mexico Historical Marker located in present-day Lordsburg (Short Park off of W 2nd Street near W Railway Boulevard -- approximate coordinates N32° 20' 60.00", W108° 43' 1.00"), indicates Lordsburg as having been **near** the Butterfield route. That marker makes a rather cryptic mention of Shakespeare in connection with the Butterfield Route. It states: "Lordsburg was founded in 1880 on the route of the Southern Pacific Railroad, **near** that used by the Butterfield Overland Mail Company, 1858-1861. It eventually absorbed most of the population of Shakespeare, a now-deserted mining town three miles south."

In a March, 2010, telephone interview Hackler maintained that the Shakespeare / Mexican Springs sites cannot be properly documented as Butterfield Station sites.

Mitigating that position, however, he also noted that the Butterfield Line may have used alternative locations in the area depending upon who had available water on any given trip. Hackler also notes that water at Barney's may not have been reliable and the topography of the area may have made approaches to the site difficult to access during rainy seasons.

Another New Mexico Historical Marker located at Shakespeare NM notes that "After a silver strike in 1869, a townsite was laid out **at the old stage stop** of Mexican Springs ...," clearly indicting that the stagecoach station there was "old" as of 1869.

Shakespeare townsite is now a privately operated ghost town attraction. Weekend tours are offered, but finding them open during the week reportedly can be somewhat "catch as catch can." Shakespeare is listed on the National Register of Historic Places (1973 - #73001141). It is located at coordinates N32° 19' 29.05", W108° 44' 17.93".

Despite his questions about Shakespeare / Mexican Springs, Hackler did visit and document the site. He locates the site of "Mexican Springs" slightly to the south and east of the Shakespeare location (approximate coordinates N32° 19' 03", W108° 43' 18").

As of October 28, 2010 correspondence, Wray indicated that OCTA research notes that Mexican Springs may have been a short-lived Butterfield stop that was quickly replaced by the Shakespeare location, although the Wray / OCTA mapping data does not include the Shakespeare / Mexican Springs spur route.

References:

Bailey, Goddard; *California -- Arrival of the Overland Mail -- Itinerary of the Route*; as reported by newspaper article; New York Times (NY) - October 14, 1858

Bailey, Goddard; *Report to Postmaster A.V. Brown - Full itinerary as reported by De Bow's Review and Industrial Resources, Statistics etc*; published by De Bow's Review; New Orleans and Washington City; 1858. See specifically *Internal Improvements - 1. Wagon Road to the Pacific*; pp 719-721. Internet accessible at http://books.google.com/books?id=5CYoAAAAYAAJ&pg=PA720&lpg=PA720&dq=Cienega+de+los+Pimas&source=bl&ots=_5lZw_Bq23&sig=T6scCb8cpbY7KwjxpYoNvZpcgvI&hl=en&ei=i6KnS6KNOIr2M5yprIED&sa=X&oi=book_result&ct=result&resnum=2&ved=0CAwQ6AEwAQ#v=onepage&q=Cienega%20de%20los%20Pimas&f=false (accessed March 22, 2010)

Conkling, Roscoe P. and Margaret B.; *The Butterfield Overland Mail, 1857–1869* (3 vols); Glendale, CA: A. H. Clark Company, 1947.

Fugate, Francis L. & Roberta B. Fugate; *Roadside History of New Mexico*; Mountain Press Publishing Company; Missoula MT; 1989

Greene, A.C.; *900 Miles On the Butterfield Trail*; University of North Texas Press; 1994

Hackler, George; *The Butterfield Trail in New Mexico*; Yucca Enterprises; Las Cruces NM; 2005

Julyan, Robert; *The Place Names of New Mexico*; University of New Mexico Press; Albuquerque; 1998

Matt, Don & Paul Matt; *The Great Butterfield Stage Expedition*; Internet publication; http://butterfieldoverlandmail.blogspot.com (accessed Jan 20, 2010).

National Register of Historic Places; *National Register Locations by State*; Internet publication; accessible at

http://www.nationalregisterofhistoricplaces.com/state.html (accessed May 3, 2010)

Oregon - California Trails Association; *Learn. Connect. Preserve.*; Internet publication accessible at http://www.octa-trails.org/ (accessed October 9, 2010)

Ormsby, Waterman L.; *The Butterfield Overland Mail (Only Through Passenger on the First Westbound Stage)*; original publications New York Herald (NY) Sep 26 - Nov 19, 1858; republished by Henry E. Huntington Library and Art Gallery, San Marino CA, 1942 - 1998

Mexican Springs / Shakespeare to Steins Pass

April 19, 2011

Shakespeare, NM - southwest of Lordsburg, NM • Hidalgo County (N32° 19' 29.05", W108° 44' 17.93")

TO Steins Pass - Steins, NM • Hidalgo County (N32° 20' 17", W109° 01' 40.00")

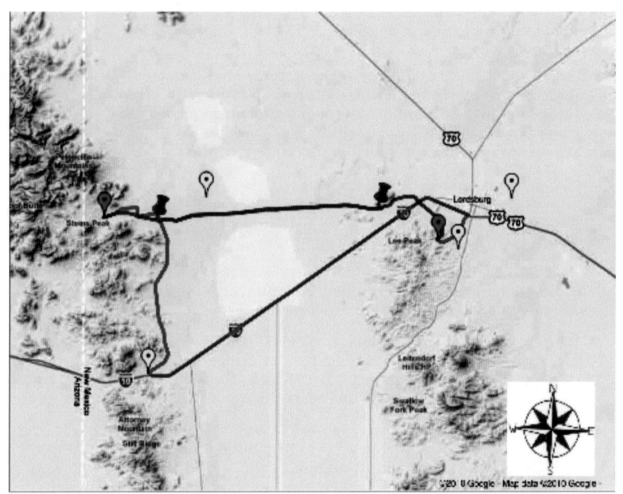

Approximate Actual Route Shakespeare to Steins 19 miles.

(No exact comparable. 1858 Bailey itinerary says 42 miles Soldiers Farewell to Steins.)

Secondary Landmarks:

"Orphaned segment" identified as Butterfield Trail on current maps - begin coordinates N32° 21' 02.71", W108° 47' 27.57" / end coordinates N32° 20' 19.51", W108° 58' 51.62"

NE mouth of Doubtful Canyon - approximate coordinates N32° 21' 21.29", W108° 56' 27.20"

Steins Ghost Town - approximate coordinates N32° 13' 45.00", W108° 59' 22.00"

Steins Peak - approximate coordinates N32° 20' 1.28", W109° 2' 37.21"

Notes:

In historical terms, the ongoing Butterfield route from Lordsburg / Shakespeare diverged from the Mormon Battalion route of 1846 - 1847. The Mormon Battalion route from the vicinity of Lordsburg / Shakespeare dropped south into Mexico while the Butterfield continues on a westward course.

The Butterfield Route through this segment continues along the course followed by the San Antonio - San Diego Stage route established by Skillman, Wasson, Birch et al. (1857).

In modern terms, George Hackler has also done substantial field research regarding this route and the station locations. The Matt Brothers did not investigate the Steins Pass route.

The Oregon - California Trails Association (OCTA) has done a significant amount of field research and mapping of this segment. That data, supplied by Chris Wray of OCTA on October 28, 2010, has also been taken into account in the preparation of this report and related map.

Mapping data supplied by Wray / OCTA confirms the mapped route westward from Barney's Station / Lordsburg but does not include the Shakespeare / Mexican Spring locations.

Slightly west of Lordsburg there is another "orphaned segment" of road identified as "Butterfield Trail" on modern maps. Whether the Butterfield coaches originated at Barney's Station or at Shakespeare / Mexican Springs in the Lordsburg area, that 11-mile stretch obviously constitutes much of the track from the Lordsburg / Shakespeare NM area westward to Steins Pass. That segment begins at approximate coordinates N32° 21' 02.71", W108° 47'

27.57" and terminates in the vicinity of coordinates N32° 20' 19.51", W108° 58' 51.62".

The last Butterfield Station within New Mexico proper is listed as Steins Pass, which was earlier known as "Doubtful Canyon." The "Doubtful" name reportedly arose as the frequent occurrence of Apache attacks on emigrant travelers through the area made it "doubtful" that the pass could be used on any given trip through the area.

By the time of the Butterfield, however, the area was also referred to as "Steins Pass" or "Steins Peak" in honor of Captain Enoch Steins, a US Cavalry officer who served in the area -- and was eventually killed during a confrontation with Apache Indians in 1873.

Bailey notes this station as "Steins Peak" as does Ormsby.

Hackler's research agrees with others that the likely location of the Steins Pass station was located in Doubtful Canyon (approximate coordinates N32° 20' 17", W109° 01' 40").

The mapping data supplied by Wray / OCTA concurs with Hackler's coordinates.

Julyan's notes regarding Steins Pass state that the pass was at the southwest mouth of Doubtful Canyon, while "The East Garrison Relay Station at the east end of the Canyon was a garrison of soldiers who accompanied westbound travelers. The station was used into the 1870s, but eventually it was abandoned." Julyan does not date this "East Garrison" station site.

Modern satellite mapping indicates the easterly mouth of Doubtful Canyon to be in the vicinity of coordinates N32° 21' 21.29", W108° 56' 27.20" with the canyon running in a south to westerly arc. That data appears to correlate Julyan's location for Steins Pass proper as being to the west of Hackler's location for Steins Pass Station within the canyon.

The Steins Peak promontory is located slightly southwest of the Butterfield Station location at approximate coordinates N32° 20' 1.28", W109° 2' 37.21".

Bailey specifically identifies "Steins Peak" as a Butterfield station location, placing it 42 miles from Soldier's Farewell.

Ormsby also mentions Steins Peak Station being 42 miles from Soldiers' Farewell, noting that "The location of the station was in a little hollow under the mountain, so that we could not see it until we were within a few hundred yards of it." Ormsby also places the station site to the east of the heart of Steins Pass / Doubtful Canyon.

Lest there be confusion, there was a post-Butterfield community established in this vicinity and named Steins.

Just off of Interstate 10 at Steins Road, the post-Butterfield site of the late-1800s town of Steins is now another private-enterprise ghost town location that helps to serve as a locator for the Butterfield site, but only as a landmark.

The Fugates state specifically that "The railroad town of Steins or Steins Pass is not to be confused with Steins Station or Steins Pass on the Butterfield Overland Mail route. The latter are on private land some 14 miles north of the town of Steins."

The townsite of "Steins" (to the south of Steins Peak proper; approximate coordinates N32° 13' 45.00", W108° 59' 22.00") is interesting in and of itself even though it bears no particular relevance to Butterfield. It was established around 1900 when Southern Pacific Railroad workers established a camp in the vicinity. It should also be noted, however, that as late as 1888 the post office for this area retained the "Doubtful Canyon" name.

The town of Steins eventually boasted a water tower, coaling station and work camp named to the railroad preference. It had 35 registered voters and its own schoolhouse by 1902. Nearby mining camps also helped to fuel business development. By 1919 the population (depending on which source one chooses to believe) was between 200 and 1300 and was home to several businesses including a boarding house, two bordellos, a dance hall, a general store, one hotel, and three saloons.

The mines eventually played out and the importance of the railroad waned -- as did the town of Steins. By 1944, the post office had closed and by 1955, with the demise of coal-powered steam trains, the railroad station was shut down.

A New Mexico Historical marker just north of the ghost town site (toward the proper location of the Butterfield-era Steins Station location) reads: "This was once a bustling railroad station town supporting 1,000 residents during its peak of prosperity. The first station at Steins was built in 1858 by the Butterfield Overland Mail County. Steins Peak Station got its name from a mountain named for Major Enoch Steins, a member of the U.S. Dragoons who camped there. Steins Pass served East - and Westbound wagon trains in the 1800s. The ghost town lies near Doubtful Canyon, known for its Indian massacres."

References:

Bailey, Goddard; *California -- Arrival of the Overland Mail -- Itinerary of the Route*; as reported by newspaper article; New York Times (NY) - October 14, 1858

Bailey, Goddard; *Report to Postmaster A.V. Brown - Full itinerary as reported by De Bow's Review and Industrial Resources, Statistics etc;* published by De Bow's Review; New Orleans and Washington City; 1858. See specifically *Internal Improvements - 1. Wagon Road to the Pacific*; pp 719-721. Internet accessible at
http://books.google.com/books?id=5CYoAAAAYAAJ&pg=PA720&lpg=PA720&dq=Cienega+de+los+Pimas&source=bl&ots=_5lZw_Bq23&sig=T6scCb8cpbY7KwjxpYoNvZpcgvI&hl=en&ei=i6KnS6KNOIr2M5yprIED&sa=X&oi=book_result&ct=result&resnum=2&ved=0CAwQ6AEwAQ#v=onepage&q=Cienega%20de%20los%20Pimas&f=false (accessed March 22, 2010)

Conkling, Roscoe P. and Margaret B.; *The Butterfield Overland Mail, 1857–1869* (3 vols); Glendale, CA: A. H. Clark Company, 1947.

Fugate, Francis L. & Roberta B. Fugate; *Roadside History of New Mexico*; Mountain Press Publishing Company; Missoula MT; 1989

Hackler, George; *The Butterfield Trail in New Mexico*; Yucca Enterprises; Las Cruces NM; 2005

Julyan, Robert; *The Place Names of New Mexico*; University of New Mexico Press; Albuquerque; 1998

Matt, Don & Paul Matt; *The Great Butterfield Stage Expedition*; Internet publication; http://butterfieldoverlandmail.blogspot.com (accessed Jan 20, 2010).

Oregon - California Trails Association; *Learn. Connect. Preserve.*; Internet publication accessible at http://www.octa-trails.org/ (accessed October 9, 2010)

Ormsby, Waterman L.; *The Butterfield Overland Mail (Only Through Passenger on the First Westbound Stage)*; original publications New York Herald (NY) Sep 26 - Nov 19, 1858; republished by Henry E. Huntington Library and Art Gallery, San Marino CA, 1942 – 1998.

Steins Pass (New Mexico) to Apache Springs (Arizona)

April 19, 2011

Steins Pass - Steins, NM • Hidalgo County (N32° 20' 17", W109° 01' 40.00")

TO Apache Pass / Apache Springs Station / Fort Bowie National Historic Site - south of Bowie, AZ • Cochise County (N32° 9' 24.46", W109° 27' 10.27")

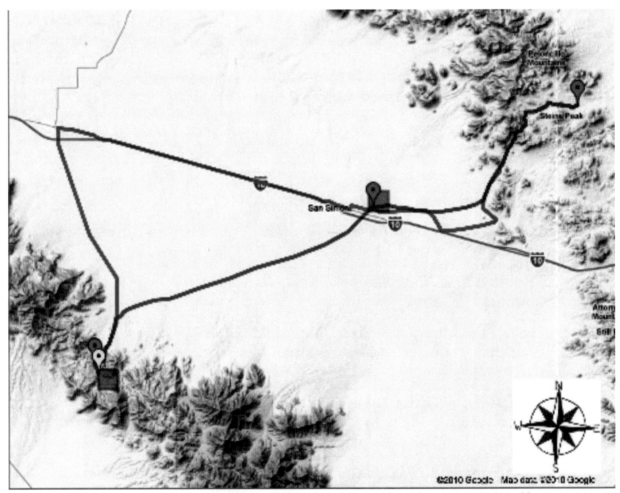

Approximate actual route Steins to Apache Pass 31.75 miles.

(1858 Bailey itinerary says 35 miles)

75

Secondary Landmarks:

San Simon Station per Talbot and Ahnert - approximate coordinates N32° 17' 37.05", W109° 13' 20.36"

Notes:

In historical terms, the Butterfield Route through this segment follows the San Antonio - San Diego Stage route established by Skillman, Wasson, Birch et al (1857).

In modern terms, this segment has been well-researched and established. Hackler describes this segment in some detail.

Additionally, Gerald Ahnert (*Retracing the Butterfield Overland Trail through Arizona; a Guide to the Route of 1857-1861;* Westernlore Press; Tucson AZ; 1973) and Don Talbot (*Historical Guide to the Mormon Battalion and Butterfield Trail;* Western Lore Press; 1992) have researched and mapped this segment.

It should also be noted that Ahnert has continued his field research to include GPS readings at the various station sites and has revised and elaborated many of his earlier published findings although the more recent findings have not yet been published. • Note update as of March 2013 • After this report was completed, Gerald Ahnert published an updated study titled *The Butterfield Trail and Overland Mail Company in Arizona 1858-1861* (Canastota Publishing; Canastota NY; 2011). That information adds interpretive detail but agrees with the earlier findings as regards the route and stations.

Talbot and Ahnert both include a substantial number of route segment maps in their publications.

The Oregon - California Trails Association (OCTA) has also done a significant amount of field research and mapping of this segment. That data, supplied by Chris Wray of OCTA on October 28, 2010, has also been taken into account.

There was an intermediate Butterfield station site built between Steins Pass and Apache Pass at San Simon Creek.

The Conklings identify San Simon as a station location. Hackler mentions San Simon but does not pinpoint a location. In his notes regarding the route from Steins Pass to Apache Spring, Hackler states "The Doubtful Canyon Road west of the [Steins] station is made up of three parts; one mile of narrow wash, one and a half miles of gently rising broad meadow, and three miles of deep rock wall canyon ending at the Rooster Comb where it opens to the smooth descent to San Simon."

Hackler's route description appears to indicate a southwesterly route from Steins Pass to San Simon. Talbot, Ahnert and Wray / OCTA map the same southwesterly track.

In his book, Talbot states of the onward route, "A great deal of the road ... was built or improved by Col. James B. Leach. On February 17, 1857, Congress appropriated $200,000 for improving the road between El Paso and Fort Yuma. Leach was appointed to supervise this project and was assisted by Major N.H. Hutton. The work was completed in September, 1858. Two miles northeast of San Simon Station, the mail road diverged southwest of Leach's road ..."

Leach's / San Antonio - San Diego road appears the be what Postmaster General A.V. Brown referred to as "...the new road being opened and constructed under the direction of the Secretary of the Interior, [from El Paso TX] to Fort Yuma, California" in his 1857 general outline for the establishment of the Overland Mail Route.

As to the site of the San Simon Station, Talbot reports that it is located "... on the east bank of San Simon Creek just north of the Southern Pacific Railroad tracks. Nothing remains of the station today."

Talbot's detailed placement of locations in Arizona uses township, range and section citations rather than latitude and longitude. He places the San Simon Station at Township 13S, Range 31E, Section 29. Talbot's description translated to latitude and longitude places the San Simon Station in the vicinity of coordinates N32° 17' 37", W109° 13' 20".

Talbot's placement of the San Simon Station meshes closely with that reported by Gerald Ahnert. In correspondence dated October 22, 2010, Ahnert noted that the report coordinates (N32° 17' 37.05", W109° 13' 20.36") are within 1.2 miles of the specific location he has identified for the San Simon Station site in his later research, but given upcoming publication plans, did not specify comparative coordinates.

The Wray / OCTA mapping data for the San Simon Station concurs with Hackler's general description, placing the actual station site off the existing road slightly southeast of the report location, at coordinates N32° 15' 59.06", W109° 12' 23.83"

The ongoing Butterfield Route continues a generally southwesterly course across a plain into the mountains in the immediate vicinity of Apache Springs. This route is clearly mapped in modern terms by Ahnert, Talbot and the Wray / OCTA mapping data.

Apache Springs is a live water source to this day, but even the Butterfield travelers complained about the quality of the water.

The Butterfield Station site at Apache Springs is another that eventually became the site of a frontier military installation -- namely Fort Bowie. Fort Bowie was declared a National Historic Site in 1964 and placed on the National Register of Historic Places in 1972 (1972 - #72000194; 12 miles south of Bowie, AZ).

Ahnert (1973) identifies the location of the Butterfield Station as Township 15S, Range 28E, Section 12 (as does Talbot). Hackler specifies coordinates N32° 08'56", W109° 26' 57", which places the site in the northwest corner of the section as described by Ahnert and Talbot.

In correspondence on October 22, 2010, Ahnert confirmed the location of these coordinates as being within 156 feet of the updated GPS coordinates he has logged for the station.

The mapping data supplied by Wray / OCTA concurs with Hackler's placement of the actual station site.

Fort Bowie was established in 1862 on the Apache Springs site and played a pivotal role in the pursuit of Cochise and the Chiricahua Apaches. After Cochise's surrender in 1886 the fort was no longer necessary, and by 1894 the post had been completely abandoned. Thereafter, local residents salvaged the location for doorframes, windows and other materials which led to a rapid deterioration and collapse of the adobe structures.

From the parking lot at the National Historic Site, it is about a 1.5 mile hike to the site of the original fort. The hiking trail passes the ruins of the Butterfield station house. The trail also passes the post cemetery, an Apache wickiup and the foundation ruins of the old Chiricahua Apache Indian Agency once occupied by Tom Jeffords. Jeffords was a superintendent for the Overland Mail Company who negotiated a workable peace with Cochise under which the Chiricahuas agreed not to molest the Butterfield coaches as they passed through the area. Cochise and Jeffords became friends, and Jeffords was eventually appointed as the Indian agent and liaison between the United States and the Chiricahuas.

Ormsby and Bailey both identify this station as Apache Pass. Greene and the Matt Brothers also discuss Apache Pass.

Regarding the Butterfield Route through Arizona in general; in correspondence during mid-September, 2010, Ahnert indicated that the older research on the Butterfield route through Arizona is very inaccurate.

Those inaccuracies, he says, originated with the Conklings -- whom he notes did not do a thorough job of studying the historical records of the trail. Rather, he notes, the Conklings' findings in Arizona relied on anecdotal information that was not verified according to historical records.

"There is little of the Conklings book that is correct about Arizona," Ahnert wrote. "They ... relied on people who lived in the area of the stations (in the 1930s). ... There was no one alive at the time who could act with any credibility on locating the original Butterfield stations. Most [stations] were destroyed or replaced."

Given Ahnert's criticism of past research, particular effort and attention should be given to the Arizona route during in-depth Trail Planning and Implementation phases.

References:

Ahnert, Gerald T.; *Retracing the Butterfield Overland Trail through Arizona; a Guide to the Route of 1857-1861;* Westernlore Press; Tucson AZ; 1973 and *The Butterfield Trail and Overland Mail Company in Arizona 1858-1861*; Canastota Publishing; Canastota NY; 2011

Bailey, Goddard; *California -- Arrival of the Overland Mail -- Itinerary of the Route*; as reported by newspaper article; New York Times (NY) - October 14, 1858

Bailey, Goddard; *Report to Postmaster A.V. Brown - Full itinerary as reported by De Bow's Review and Industrial Resources, Statistics etc;* published by De Bow's Review; New Orleans and Washington City; 1858. See specifically *Internal Improvements - 1. Wagon Road to the Pacific*; pp 719-721. Internet accessible at http://books.google.com/books?id=5CYoAAAAYAAJ&pg=PA720&lpg=PA720& dq=Cienega+de+los+Pimas&source=bl&ots=_5lZw_Bq23&sig=T6scCb8cpbY7K wjxpYoNvZpcgvI&hl=en&ei=i6KnS6KNOIr2M5yprIED&sa=X&oi=book_result& ct=result&resnum=2&ved=0CAwQ6AEwAQ#v=onepage&q=Cienega%20de%20 los%20Pimas&f=false (accessed March 22, 2010)

Conkling, Roscoe P. and Margaret B.; *The Butterfield Overland Mail, 1857–1869* (3 vols); Glendale, CA: A. H. Clark Company, 1947.

Earthpoint; *Township and Range, Public Land Survey System on Google Earth*; internet data conversion system accessible at http://www.earthpoint.us/townships.aspx (accessed April 22, 2010)

Greene, A.C.; *900 Miles On the Butterfield Trail*; University of North Texas Press; 1994

Hackler, George; *The Butterfield Trail in New Mexico*; Yucca Enterprises; Las Cruces NM; 2005

Matt, Don & Paul Matt; *The Great Butterfield Stage Expedition*; Internet publication; http://butterfieldoverlandmail.blogspot.com (accessed Jan 20, 2010)

National Register of Historic Places; *National Register Locations by State*; Internet publication; accessible at

http://www.nationalregisterofhistoricplaces.com/state.html (accessed May 3, 2010)

Oregon - California Trails Association; *Learn. Connect. Preserve.*; Internet publication accessible at http://www.octa-trails.org/ (accessed October 9, 2010)

Ormsby, Waterman L.; *The Butterfield Overland Mail (Only Through Passenger on the First Westbound Stage)*; original publications New York Herald (NY) Sep 26 - Nov 19, 1858; republished by Henry E. Huntington Library and Art Gallery, San Marino CA, 1942 - 1998

Talbot, Don; *Historical Guide to the Mormon Battalion and Butterfield Trail;* Western Lore Press, 1992

Apache Springs to Ewell's Spring

April 19, 2011

Apache Pass / Apache Springs Station / Fort Bowie National Historic Site - south of Bowie, AZ • Cochise County (N32° 9'24.46", W109° 27' 10.27")

TO Ewell Spring southwest of Dos Cabezas AZ • Cochise County(N32 07' 36.13", W109 39' 00.38")

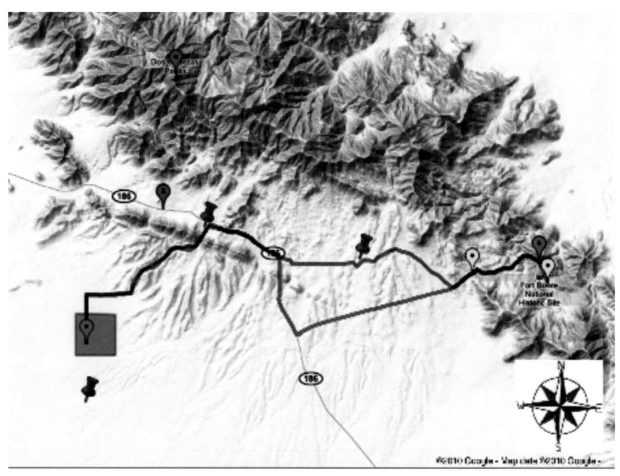

Approximate actual route Apache Pass to Ewell Spring 11 miles.

(1858 Bailey itinerary does not mention Ewell Spring - through mileage to Dragoon Springs = 40 miles)

Secondary Landmarks:

Dos Cabezas (community) - approximate coordinates N32° 10' 31.08", W109° 37' 0.87"

Dos Cabezas Peaks (geological formation) - approximate coordinates N32° 13' 24.28", W109° 36' 40.23"

"Butterfield Trail" segment - east and south of Dos Cabezas AZ - begin coordinates N32° 9' 25.92", W109° 31' 42.81" / end coordinates N32° 10' 8.73", W109° 35' 46.85"

Notes:

While there may be some available confusion regarding the site of the Butterfield station at Dos Cabezas / Ewell Spring, the Butterfield route is fairly "cut and dried."

In historical terms, the route along the early road was improved by Col. James B. Leach (1857) and used by the San Antonio - San Diego Stageline established by Skillman, Wasson, Birch et al (1857).

Neither Ormsby nor Bailey indicate an intermediary stop along the 40-mile traverse between Apache Springs and Dragoon Springs as of 1858, however. Bailey's itinerary reports this overall segment as having been "without water" from Apache Spring to Dragoon Spring.

Reports by later Butterfield travelers do clearly indicate an intermediate station stop as of 1859 -1861.

In modern terms, Talbot and Ahnert (1973) include relatively small-scale detail maps of the immediate Ewell Spring Station area that do not give a particularly clear "big picture" of the overall route.

During the process of preparing this segment, however, Gerald Ahnert was supplied with a preliminary draft of the findings contained herein and related map for review. Ahnert's suggestions and comments on the routing and site locations have been taken into account in the preparation of this report.

The Oregon - California Trails Association (OCTA) has also done a significant amount of field research and mapping of this segment. That data; supplied by Chris Wray of OCTA as of October 28, 2010; has also been taken into account. The detailed Wray / OCTA mapping data clearly indicates the westerly to southwesterly route as outlined in this segment map.

Much of the route through this segment can also be identified on modern maps, listed as "Butterfield Road". That segment begins slightly west of Apache Springs (begin coordinates N32° 9' 25.92", W109° 31' 42.81") and continues west following E Stagecoach Road into Arizona Highway 186. At Rancho Sacatal Road, this "Butterfield Road" then drops to the south and west via Jeffords Trail, Indian Trail and Covered Wagon Road. The "Butterfield Road" segment terminates slightly south of the Talbot / Ahnert / Conkling location for Ewell's Station (end coordinates N32° 6' 18.07", W109° 38' 59.91").

The intermediate stop variously referred to as "Dos Cabezas" and as "Ewell's Spring" by travelers after 1858 clearly indicate this station site as being a Butterfield Station.

According to some sources, this stage station was initially built for the San Antonio and San Diego Stage Line.

By those reports, the station "at Dos Cabezas" (Spanish meaning "Two Heads") was established in 1857. By 1858, many of the San Antonio and San Diego routes and stations became part of the Butterfield Overland contract. Thus it is possible-to-likely that latter Butterfield routings "broke" the harrowing 40-mile desert segment to Dragoon Springs with water stops at Dos Cabezas / Ewell's when the redundant San Antonio - San Diego postal contract lapsed.

Herein lies the confusion. The simple descriptor "at Dos Cabezas" appears to be applicable to three different locations:

• The present mapped community of Dos Cabezas AZ (approximate coordinates N32° 10' 31.08", W109° 37' 0.87");

• The geological feature known as Dos Cabezas Peaks just north of the present community (approximate coordinates N32° 13' 24.28", W109° 36' 40.23"); and

• A station site also identified as Ewell's Spring just south of the present community (approximate coordinates N32 07' 36.13", W109 39' 00.38").

While it appears likely that the Butterfield Station was indeed at the southwesterly Ewell's Spring site, we will deal with all three locations.

According to the website mycohise.com, maintained by the Cochise County AZ Genealogical Society, Ewell's Spring and Ewell's Station may have been synonymous with the site at Dos Cabezas. Apparently following the lead of researcher Byrd Howell Granger in *Arizona's Names - X Marks the Place,*

Historical Names of Places in Arizona (Falconer Publishing Company, 1983), Ewell's Spring was "an early name for Dos Cabezas."

Ewell's Station, mycochise.com reports, "was a relay route between Apache Pass and Dragoon Springs. Probably the location of Ewell's Spring and Dos Cabezas."

That research also indicates the station at Dos Cabezas did not fare well in the long run. By 1861 the station had been abandoned by Butterfield and destroyed by the Apaches. Various reports indicate that in the early 1860s (post-Butterfield), twenty-seven mail carriers were killed by the Indians along the route between Apache Springs / Fort Bowie and Ewell's Station.

According to Don Talbot in his *Historical Guide to the Mormon Battalion and Butterfield Trail*, (Western Lore Press 1992), the first Arizona station after Apache Springs was at Ewell's Spring / Ewell's Station. Talbot puts Ewell's Station "about five miles south of Dos Cabezas ... on the private property of El Paso Natural Gas Company."

As of 1992, Talbot notes "Nothing remains there today." The adobe station, he reports, was built in early 1859 and "named for Captain R.S. Ewell of the First Dragoons, one of the founders of Fort Buchanan (established 1856, approximately 15 miles southwest of Ewell's)."

Specifically, Talbot places Ewell's Station within Township 15S, Range 26E, Section 13 near the boundary with Township 15S Range 26E, Section 14 [toward the west]. This location mirrors Ahnert's placement as of 1973.

Translated to latitude and longitude, that description places Ewell's Station toward the southwestern corner of boundaries as follows:

Section S13 T15S R26E

Meridian Gila-Salt River

State Arizona

Source BLM

Calculated Values

Acres 641

Centroid 32.1303484, -109.6458593

Corners NW 32.1376010, -109.6544138

NE 32.1375905, -109.6373674

SE 32.1231027, -109.6373148

SW 32.1230980, -109.6543543

The Ewell's Spring station location described by the Conklings appears to correlate to the same vicinity as cited by Ahnert and Talbot.

Using Talbot's description and the Conklings' location compared to Ahnert's data, approximate coordinates for this site would be in the vicinity of N32 07' 36.13", W109 39' 00.38" -- which coordinates we have used for the purpose of this report. In correspondence as of September 22, 2010, Ahnert places this location as being within 600 feet of his most recent coordinate notation.

The Wray / OCTA mapping data specifically places Ewell Spring at coordinates N32° 7' 35.37", W109° 39' 15.76" (approximately .3 mile west of the report coordinates).

As to the possibility of a station directly at Dos Cabezas Peaks, it is highly unlikely that the Butterfield coaches would have scaled the peaks themselves.

Regarding the modern community of Dos Cabezas AZ at the southern foot of the peaks, mycochise.com and other resources indicate that location was not a proper settlement until the late-1870s.

While the first American mining claims in the Dos Cabezas area were filed by several soldiers turned prospectors in 1864. Silver and gold mining activities brought the former station location to status as a small town by 1878.

The town of Dos Cabezas was first settled in 1878 and named for the two bald peaks visible nearby. The community had its own post office as of April 8, 1879. It was closed on January 31, 1960. During the early 1900s, Dos Cabezas served as an "R&R" location for soldiers posted at nearby Fort Bowie. However, most of the population left after a 1916 drought ended agriculture in the area and 1926 saw closure of the last of the mining operations in the area.

Descriptions of the early settlement indicate the town had a barber shop, a brewery, a general store, brick yard, hotel, blacksmith, and about 300 people in the late 1870s. Dos Cabezas still exists but is essentially a ghost town. Several of the old structures still exist but are little more than abandoned ruins.

It should be noted that the "Butterfield Road" route and the route as delineated in the Wray / OCTA mapping data bypasses both the community of Dos Cabezas and Dos Cabezas Peaks well to the east and south of those locations.

References:

Ahnert, Gerald T.; *Retracing the Butterfield Overland Trail through Arizona; a Guide to the Route of 1857-1861;* Westernlore Press; Tucson AZ;1973

Cochise County (AZ) Genealogical Society; *Cochise County Place Names*; Internet accessible at http://www.mycochise.com/placenames.php (Accessed July 3, 2010)

Conkling, Roscoe P. and Margaret B.; *The Butterfield Overland Mail,1857–1869* (Three Volumes); Glendale, CA: A. H. Clarke Company, 1947.

Earthpoint; *Township and Range, Public Land Survey System on Google Earth*; internet data conversion system accessible at http://www.earthpoint.us/townships.aspx (accessed April 22, 2010

Granger, Byrd Howell; *Arizona's Names - X Marks the Place, Historical Names of Places in Arizona;* Falconer Publishing Company, 1983

Oregon - California Trails Association; *Learn. Connect. Preserve.*; Internet publication accessible at http://www.octa-trails.org/ (accessed October 9, 2010)

Talbot, Don; *Historical Guide to the Mormon Battalion and Butterfield Trail;* Western Lore Press, 1992

Ewell's Spring to Dragoon Spring

April 20, 2011

Ewell's Springs • Cochise County (N32° 7' 36.13", W109° 39' 00.38")

TO Dragoon Springs - Dragoon, AZ • Cochise County (N31° 59' 51.10", W110° 1' 20.50")

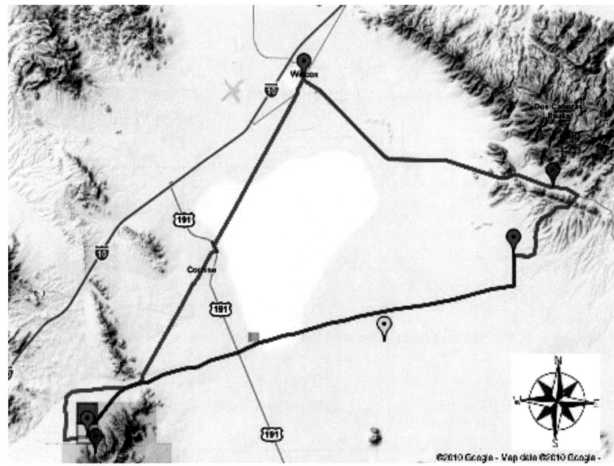

Approximate Actual Route, Ewell's Springs to Dragoon Springs 25 miles (1858 Bailey itinerary does not mention Ewell's Springs - through mileage Apache Springs to Dragoon Springs = 40 miles)

Secondary Landmarks:

Willcox - approximate coordinates N32° 15' 11.06", W109° 49' 55.60"

Kansas Settlement - approximate coordinates N32° 3' 54.30", W109° 45' 46.23"

Notes:

The Butterfield Route through this segment diverges substantially from the modern roads and is, in part, inaccessible.

In historical terms, the continuing Butterfield Route continues along the early road as improved by Col. James B. Leach (1857) and used by the San Antonio - San Diego Stages established by Skillman, Wasson, Birch et al. (1857).

In the modern context, Talbot (1992) and Ahnert (1973) include detailed maps of the immediate Ewell's Springs to Dragoon Springs route. Compared to one another, those maps clearly indicate the southwesterly route from Ewell's Springs passing just to the north of Kansas Settlement and continuing southwestward across the Willcox Playa to Dragoon Springs.

The Oregon - California Trails Association (OCTA) has also done a significant amount of field research and mapping of this segment. That data; supplied by Chris Wray of OCTA as of October 28, 2010; has also been taken into account. The detailed Wray / OCTA mapping data clearly indicates the southwesterly route as outlined in this segment map.

The inaccessible portion of this segment on the original route lies toward the southwest from Kansas Settlement (approximate coordinates N32° 3' 54.30", W109° 45' 46.23") through to an intersection with what is now U.S. Highway 191. That segment lies within the confines of the former Willcox Dry Lake Bombing Range used to train bombardiers, navigators, pilots and other military aircraft personnel. It is a clearly-marked restricted military area. It is closed to the public in part due to the presence of unexploded ordnance that would constitute a safety threat if the former target area were publicly accessible.

Willcox Dry Lake is one of two areas where the original Butterfield Route is inaccessible due to passage through a former bombing range target area. The other such location is near the Carrizo Creek Station / Anza Borrego Desert State Park in California.

This inaccessibility forces the auto route between these stations to take a wide detour to the north via Willcox.

Some local research indicates that Willcox was a stop "on the Overland Mail" route. However, a routing from Apache Springs to Dragoon Springs via Willcox proper makes the overall journey some 58 miles -- as compared to Bailey's measurement of 40 miles between those stations.

Willcox (originally known as "Maley") was founded in 1880 as a whistle stop on the Southern Pacific Railroad. In 1889 it was renamed in honor of a visit by General Orlando B. Willcox. Willcox had served the Union Army with distinction at the Battle of Bull Run and also served as Commander of the Military Department of Arizona. General Willcox was a passenger on the first train to arrive at the town.

Willcox grew to prominence as a cattle town and remains vibrant today. Henry Hooker's Sierra Bonita ranch was one of the first large scale ranches in the area. The Headquarters Saloon in Willcox was the site of the killing of Wyatt Earp's youngest brother, Warren Earp, on July 6, 1900 at the age of 45. Warren Earp is buried in the Old Willcox Cemetery.

Clearly, the Butterfield Route crossed the Sulphur Springs Valley / Willcox Playa well to the south of the latter town of Willcox. The Sulphur Springs Valley / Willcox Playa cuts a northwesterly swath through Cochise County for nearly 100 miles. The Sulphur Springs Valley is a relatively smooth plain that averages more than 15 miles in width. On the western verge of the Willcox Playa / Sulphur Springs Valley, the Wray / OCTA data clearly shows the "Old Dragoon Road" used by Butterfield following a southwesterly curve to the Dragoon Springs Station.

Bailey and Ormsby both specifically mention Dragoon Springs.

Situated near Cochise's main encampment in the Dragoon Mountains, the Dragoon Springs stage station had a violent history from its beginnings. Three men building the station in 1858 were reportedly beaten to death in a dispute with other laborers. Their graves, and the graves of four Confederate Arizona Rangers killed by the Apaches in an unrelated incident, are near the well-preserved stone ruins of the station.

During the Civil War, Confederate soldiers posted here had more to worry about from the Apaches than from Union soldiers. There were at least two skirmishes between Confederate troops and the Apaches at Dragoon Springs. The four soldiers buried here were involved in an 1862 skirmish.

Dragoon Springs is located in the Coronado National Forest administered by the United States Forest Service. The remains of the buildings at Dragoon Springs are fairly well preserved and can be visited.

Ahnert (1973) places the Dragoon Springs Station site as having straddled the boundary between Township 16S, Range 23E, Section 32 (as reported by Talbot) and Section 29 to the north.

Talbot (1992) cites Dragoon Springs as being within the southwestern quarter of Township 16S, Range 23E, Section 32 (slightly north of the modern GIS coordinates, but containing site coordinates reported by Bill Gillespie, Forest Archaeologist for the Coronado National Forest).

Modern GIS databases (Google Earth, etc.) place Dragoon Springs at approximate coordinates N31° 59' 05.30", W110° 0' 56.25". The specific coordinates used in this report (N31° 59' 51.10", W110° 1' 20.50") were supplied via correspondence with Bill Gillespie, Forest Archaeologist for the Coronado National Forest on September 29, 2010. Gillespie noted that the Butterfield station site was "about a half mile from the spring itself."

In correspondence as of September 22, 2010, Ahnert confirmed Gillespie's coordinates as being exactly the same as his most recent measurement. • Data update as of March, 2013 • Mr. Ahnert has also published an updated and revised study, *The Butterfield Trail and Overland Mail Company in Arizona; 1858-1861* (2011 – Canastota Publishing Co, Canastota NY). That study also confirms these coordinates for Dragoon Springs.

Coordinates cited in the Wray / OCTA data concur with those cited by Gillespie and Ahnert (2010).

References:

Ahnert, Gerald T.; *Retracing the Butterfield Overland Trail through Arizona; a Guide to the Route of 1857-1861;* Westernlore Press; Tucson AZ; 1973 and *The Butterfield Trail and Overland Mail Company in Arizona; 1858-1861*; Canastota Publishing Co, Canastota NY: 2011.

Bailey, Goddard; *California -- Arrival of the Overland Mail -- Itinerary of the Route*; as reported by newspaper article; *New York Times* (NY) - October 14, 1858.

Bailey, Goddard; *Report to Postmaster General A.V. Brown - Full itinerary as reported by De Bow's Review and Industrial Resources, Statistics etc.;* published by *De Bow's Review*; New Orleans and Washington City; 1858. See specifically *Internal Improvements - 1. Wagon Road to the Pacific*; pp. 719-721. Internet accessible at
http://books.google.com/books?id=5CYoAAAAYAAJ&pg=PA720&lpg=PA720&dq=Cienega+de+los+Pimas&source=bl&ots=_5lZw_Bq23&sig=T6scCb8cpbY7KwjxpYoNvZpcgvI&hl=en&ei=i6KnS6KNOIr2M5yprIED&sa=X&oi=book_result&

ct=result&resnum=2&ved=0CAwQ6AEwAQ#v=onepage&q=Cienega%20de%20
los%20Pimas&f=false (accessed March 22, 2010).

Conkling, Roscoe P. and Margaret B.; *The Butterfield Overland Mail, 1857–
1869* (3 vols.); Glendale, CA: A. H. Clark Company, 1947.

Earthpoint; *Township and Range, Public Land Survey System on Google
Earth*; internet data conversion system accessible at
http://www.earthpoint.us/townships.aspx (accessed April 22, 2010).

Oregon - California Trails Association; *Learn. Connect. Preserve.*; Internet
publication accessible at http://www.octa-trails.org/ (accessed October 9,
2010).

Ormsby, Waterman L.; *The Butterfield Overland Mail (Only Through
Passenger on the First Westbound Stage)*; original publications *New York
Herald* (NY) Sep 26 - Nov 19, 1858; republished by Henry E. Huntington
Library and Art Gallery, San Marino CA, 1942 – 1998.

Talbot, Dan; *Historical Guide to the Mormon Battalion and Butterfield Trail;*
Westernlore Press, 1992.

**Butterfield Station ruins at Dragoon Springs
Station, Coronado National Forest
(N31.997, W110.026). Photo by Fred Yeck (2011).**

Dragoon Spring to San Pedro Station

April 20, 2011

Dragoon Springs - Dragoon, AZ • Cochise County (N31° 59' 51.10", W110° 1' 20.50")

   TO San Pedro Crossing - Benson, AZ • Cochise County (N31° 59' 15.05", W110° 18' 25.54")

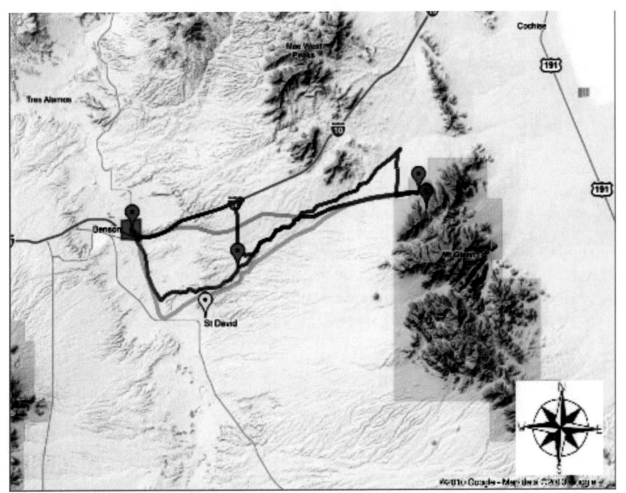

Approximate Actual Route, Dragoon Springs to San Pedro Crossing

19.25 miles (1858 Bailey itinerary = 23 miles)

Secondary Landmarks:

Saint David AZ - approximate coordinates N31 54' 25.45", W110 12' 32.04"

Notes:

The body of research to-date indicates that the Butterfield Route through this segment continued along the road improved by Col. James B. Leach (1857) and used by the San Antonio - San Diego Stages established by Skillman, Wasson, Birch et al. (1857). Unfortunately, however, no detailed description of that route has been found save that it traversed from Dragoon Spring to the San Pedro Crossing near what is now Benson.

The Butterfield route also rejoins the course of the Mormon Battalion Route (1846 - 1847) in this segment.

Ormsby wrote, "The road leads through deep gullies and beds of creeks and over walls; and once more we came to the interminable mesquite timber, looking like crab apple trees or stunted oak -- when suddenly we wheeled into the valley of the San Pedro. The stream itself is insignificant, but the valley has the appearance of having been once a vast stream of itself -- bordered as it is by bluffs of an abruptly ending plain, far above its level, on the west and sloping hills on the east. Our road led a few miles north in this valley -- in which there was not, that we could see, a respectably sized tree -- and finally crossed the stream (if by that name it might be dignified) and took a westerly course over the hills, from which we had a fine view of the San Pedro Valley."

Bailey cites the mileage along this segment as having been 23 miles.

Of some note (and worth further investigation) is that the route described by Ormsby and measured by Bailey appears to bring the Butterfield Route into close proximity of the later Mormon Community of Saint David (approximate coordinates N31° 54' 25.45", W110° 12' 32.04").

While little data has been found directly identifying Saint David as significant to the Butterfield, the eventual location of the community is known to have been explored as early as 1846 by members of the Mormon Battalion. It is well established that the Mormon Battalion came through the San Pedro Valley -- traveling north along the San Pedro River from the vicinity of Charleston AZ toward what is now Benson AZ and thence to Tucson.

During an October 3, 2010, telephone interview, Larry Ludwig of the National Park Service (Fort Bowie National Historic Site) noted that "I have heard from several researchers that the [Butterfield} route came in [to San Pedro Valley] about two miles up [north] from Saint David and then followed the valley for about three miles to the crossing. I'm not sure how much of that is based on mapping or if several different people are reading the same thing -- but there have been several mentions of that routing."

While the community of Saint David was not established until 1877, it is important to note that it was established under the leadership of Philomon Christopher Merrill (1820-1904). Merrill had been a young lieutenant with the Mormon Battalion who became an important Mormon leader, serving as a church liaison to Great Britain (1853-1856) and a key figure in the establishment of Mormon communities in Liberty and Soda Springs, Idaho in the mid-to-late 1860s. He returned to the San Pedro Valley in 1877 to facilitate the establishment of the community of Saint David. The community was named for David W. Patten, an early Mormon apostle who had been killed in 1838 in Missouri.

The identification of this area along the 1846 Mormon Battalion Route, given Ormsby's description and Bailey's mileage measure, renders strong indication that this "known point" may well have been along the route traveled by the Butterfield coaches as of 1858 -- although there is some question as to exactly where the Butterfield Route joined the Mormon Battalion Route in this area.

Also factored into this equation is that the Saint David area would have been far more attractive to the later Mormon settlers if it was located near the junction of two established roads or trails (San Pedro Valley / Mormon Battalion coming from the south and Butterfield Route essentially east-west).

Some research indicates the Butterfield route took a more westerly course, passing well to the north of Saint David. Such a route, however, crosses terrain that would have been extremely difficult to navigate for stagecoaches without substantial road improvements.

This "Northern Road," however, would have been a trek of about 15 miles -- a full eight miles short of the 23 miles recorded by Postal Inspector Goddard Bailey in his official report to Postmaster General Aaron Brown in 1858. Additionally, this more northerly route would ignore Ormsby's contention that "Our road led a few miles north in this [San Pedro River] valley..." before reaching the San Pedro crossing.

Talbot does not speak in depth about this segment, but notes that the Butterfield route traveled due-westward and joined the Mormon Battalion Route "across the river and about a mile west" of the San Pedro Station. He appears to support the more direct "North Road" as the Butterfield Route.

Ahnert (1973) maps the Butterfield Route as having taken the due-westerly "North Road" course from Dragoon Springs to San Pedro Crossing.

In conversation and correspondence on September 29, 2010, Cheryl Mammano (curator of the San Pedro Valley Arts and Historical Society in Benson) noted that the "North Road" route was most commonly assumed to have been the primary route between Dragoon Springs and San Pedro Crossing.

During an October 6, 2010, telephone interview, Rose Ann Thompkins of OCTA indicated that she felt the route tracked the more westerly "North Road" for most of the Butterfield period. She also noted, however, that there are three distinct coach roads through the area from Dragoon Springs to Benson -- the more direct "North Road", a "Middle Road" that enters the San Pedro Valley just north of Saint David, and a "Southern Road" passing directly through Saint David.

It appears likely that the "Southern Road" was probably a late-1870s route connecting the new community of Saint David directly to Dragoon and points east.

Additional research into the possible connection of the Saint David area with the Butterfield Route is needed. However, (for reasons stated,) what Thompkins suggested as the "Middle Road" appears to have been the most likely original route given Ormsby's description and Ludwig's comments.

It is conceivable that the first several trips of the Butterfield used the "Middle Road" as additional grading, leveling and other road improvements were made along the "North Road" in order to clip a few miles off of later Butterfield journeys -- quite possibly as part of the previously cited road improvements being done by Col. James B. Leach during 1857 - 1858.

In correspondence of October 20, 2010, Ahnert maintained that the "Middle Road" was, indeed, the initial Butterfield Route. He stated "For a short time after the start of the Butterfield Overland Mail Company's operation, the trail from Dragoon Springs Station, going west, went to Dragoon Wash and then followed the wash southwest to just above the present town of Saint David. It then turned west to the east bank of the San Pedro River and followed it north to the site of the San Pedro Station ... this early, longer, Butterfield Route was also the old San Antonio to San Diego Mail and Emigrant Trail." Ahnert also noted that "By late October [1858] the shorter ["North Road"] route had been established."

• Data update as of March, 2013 – Mr. Ahnert has also published an updated and revised study, *The Butterfield Trail and Overland Mail Company in Arizona; 1858-1861* (2011 – Canastota Publishing Co, Canastota NY). In that study and in several ensuing conversations, Ahnert has noted that the shorter "North Road" was most likely uncompleted in time for the first few Butterfield runs, but was used during most of the Butterfield period. Thus, both the "Middle Road" just north of St. David and the "North Road" can lay legitimate claim to being "Butterfield routes."

The Oregon - California Trails Association (OCTA) has done a significant amount of field research and mapping of this segment as well. That data; supplied by Chris Wray of OCTA as of October 28, 2010; has also been taken into account. The detailed Wray / OCTA mapping data clearly indicates the shorter westerly course along the "North Road" and does not indicate any southwesterly "dip" into the Saint David area.

The San Pedro Station at the crossing of the San Pedro River appears to have been slightly north and east of the present city of Benson -- most likely in the vicinity of Pomerene Road near Barney Drive. Unfortunately, no positive site can be cited as the station was literally wiped off the map by a flood in the area during 1883 - 1884.

Talbot places the San Pedro Crossing within Township 17S, Range 20E, Section 11 as does Ahnert (1973). Locational coordinates at N31° 59' 15.05", W110° 18' 25.54" would be near the center of the grid described by Talbot and Ahnert.

In correspondence on October 22, 2010, Ahnert placed the specific San Pedro Station coordinates "on private land ... on the east bank of the San Pedro River" about 1800 feet northwest of the report coordinates.

• Data update as of March, 2013 • Ahnert's 2011 book and data reported by researcher Fred Yeck both place the actual San Pedro Station / San Pedro Crossing just off of the public road cited for coordinates in this report. Both cite exact coordinates at N31° 58' 21.72", W110° 16' 39.72.

The Wray / OCTA mapping data concurs with the placement according to Ahnert's description (coordinates N31° 58' 20.46", W110° 16' 40.04").

The town of Benson grew after the Southern Pacific Railroad came through in the 1880s and was named for Judge William B. Benson of California -- a well-connected friend of the railroad president. It was not incorporated as a town until 1924; however, the community still celebrates "Butterfield Stage Days" each year in commemoration of the stage route.

Future research efforts regarding this segment should include additional input from Oregon - California Trails Association and the San Pedro Valley Arts & Historical Society (Benson). The San Pedro Valley Arts & Historical Society maintains an historical museum located at San Pedro and 5th Streets in Benson.

• Data update as of March 2013 • In recent correspondence, Gerald Ahnert reports that the City of Benson is considering a plan to place several markers and interpretive signage along the Butterfield route through their city.

References:

Ahnert, Gerald T.; *Retracing the Butterfield Overland Trail through Arizona; a Guide to the Route of 1857-1861;* Westernlore Press; Tucson AZ; 1973 and *The Butterfield Trail and Overland Mail Company in Arizona; 1858-1861*; Canastota Publishing Co, Canastota NY; 2011.

Bailey, Goddard; *California -- Arrival of the Overland Mail -- Itinerary of the Route*; as reported by newspaper article; *New York Times* (NY) - October 14, 1858.

Bailey, Goddard; *Report to Postmaster General A.V. Brown - Full itinerary as reported by De Bow's Review and Industrial Resources, Statistics etc.;* published by *De Bow's Review*; New Orleans and Washington City; 1858. See specifically *Internal Improvements - 1. Wagon Road to the Pacific*; pp. 719-721. Internet accessible at http://books.google.com/books?id=5CYoAAAAYAAJ&pg=PA720&lpg=PA720&dq=Cienega+de+los+Pimas&source=bl&ots=_5lZw_Bq23&sig=T6scCb8cpbY7KwjxpYoNvZpcgvI&hl=en&ei=i6KnS6KNOIr2M5yprIED&sa=X&oi=book_result&ct=result&resnum=2&ved=0CAwQ6AEwAQ#v=onepage&q=Cienega%20de%20los%20Pimas&f=false (accessed March 22, 2010).

Brown, Orson Pratt; *The Life, Times and Family of Orson Pratt Brown - Philomon Merrill*; Internet publication accessible at http://www.orsonprattbrown.com/MormonBattalion/philemon-merrill1820-1904.html (accessed July 19, 2010).

Conkling, Roscoe P. and Margaret B.; *The Butterfield Overland Mail, 1857–1869* (3 vols.); Glendale, CA: A. H. Clark Company, 1947.

Earthpoint; *Township and Range, Public Land Survey System on Google Earth*; internet data conversion system accessible at http://www.earthpoint.us/townships.aspx (accessed April 22, 2010).

Oregon - California Trails Association; *Learn. Connect. Preserve.*; Internet publication accessible at http://www.octa-trails.org/ (accessed October 9, 2010).

Ormsby, Waterman L.; *The Butterfield Overland Mail (Only Through Passenger on the First Westbound Stage)*; original publications *New York Herald* (NY) Sep 26 - Nov 19, 1858; republished by Henry E. Huntington Library and Art Gallery, San Marino CA, 1942 – 1998.

San Pedro Valley Arts & Historical Society; *Benson Museum;* Internet publication accessible at http://bensonmuseum.com/ (accessed October 9, 2010).

Talbot, Dan; *Historical Guide to the Mormon Battalion and Butterfield Trail;* Westernlore Press, 1992.

**Vicinity of San Pedro Crossing, Benson AZ (N31.972, W110.277).
Photo by Fred Yeck (2011).**

San Pedro Station to Cienega Creek Crossing

May 23, 2011

San Pedro Crossing - Benson, AZ • Cochise County (N31° 59' 15.05", W110° 18' 25.54")

TO Cienega Creek Crossing - near Vail, AZ • Pima County (N32° 01' 08.03", W110° 38' 46.48")

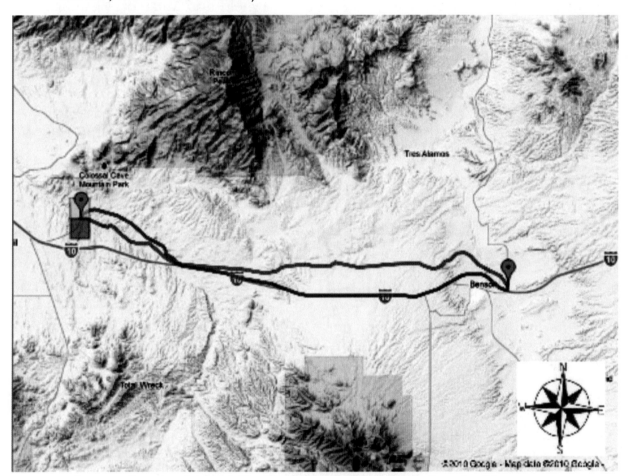

Approximate Actual Route, San Pedro Crossing to Cienega Creek 24 miles

(1858 Bailey itinerary = 24 miles)

Notes:

The ongoing Butterfield route tracks the Mormon Battalion Route of 1846 - 1847. It also follows the road improved by Col. James B. Leach (1857) and used by the San Antonio - San Diego Stages established by Skillman, Wasson, Birch et al. (1857).

In modern terms, Talbot (1992) and Ahnert (1973) include detailed maps of the immediate San Pedro Crossing to Cienega Creek route. Those maps clearly indicate an essentially westerly route via Mescal Arroyo between the two stations. Talbot clearly overlays the Butterfield and Mormon Battalion routes through this segment. The Oregon - California Trails Association (OCTA) has also done a significant amount of field research and mapping of this segment. That data, supplied by Chris Wray of OCTA as of October 28, 2010, has also been taken into account.

The detailed Wray / OCTA mapping data clearly indicates a gentle westerly / northwesterly curve along the Mescal Arroyo as outlined in this segment map.

The area now known as Vail is another Butterfield location more notable for its post-Butterfield development than as a settlement location during the late 1850s.

Most researchers note the intermediate location between the San Pedro River Crossing and Tucson as "Cienega" or "Cienaga" ("Cienega" being the correct spelling). It is also referred to in some resources as "Cienega de los Pimas."

All of the above refers to a crossing at Cienega Creek which would have been northeast of the present community of Vail (just southwest of the intersection of I-10 and State Highway 83).

The nearby town is named Vail after Walter Lennox Vail, a prosperous rancher with connections in Arizona and California who established a substantial ranch in the area in 1876 and is mentioned for landmark purposes only. There was no permanent settlement at Vail during the Butterfield Period.

Talbot notes of the Cienega Creek Station that "The Southern Pacific Railroad tracks pass directly over the old station site and very little of the large adobe buildings remains to be seen. These buildings were destroyed by fire shortly after being abandoned and were reported to be in ruins by July 1862." He places that station site in the northeast corner of Township 16S,

Range 17E, Section 30. Ahnert (1973) places the Cienega Station within the adjacent northern quadrant of Township 16S, Range 17E, Section 19.

Given the proximity of the railroad tracks to the modern course of Cienega Creek and the close similarity between the Ahnert and Talbot descriptions, the Cienega Station location would be at a presently inaccessible site slightly southwest of approximate coordinates N32° 01' 08.03", W110° 38' 46.48".

In correspondence dated October 22, 2010, Ahnert placed these coordinates as being within 1100 feet of his most recent coordinate measurement. • Data update as of March, 2013 • In his 2011 publication, Ahnert specifically identified these coordinates at N32° 1' 8.40", W110° 38' 33.72".

The Wray / OCTA mapping data concurs with the Ahnert description, placing the site at coordinates N32° 1' 12.81", W110° 38' 22.59", slightly east of the report coordinates.

• Data update as of March 2013 • Researcher Fred Yeck also reports coordinates for this station within a few feet of those cited in this report and reported according to Talbot, Ahnert and Wray / OCTA.

Ormsby noted of this station that "We ascend from the valleys of the Ciniqua, with its beautiful grass and weeds, to the mountainous district approaching Tucson, the first city in Arizona after leaving Mesilla worthy of any note. We change our horses before leaving the Ciniqua, for its heavy sand and the coming hard hills are very wearying upon the animals."

Bailey identifies this station as a mileage point, although he refers to it as "Seneca".

References:

Ahnert, Gerald T.; *Retracing the Butterfield Overland Trail through Arizona; a Guide to the Route of 1857-1861;* Westernlore Press; Tucson AZ; 1973 and *The Butterfield Trail and Overland Mail Company in Arizona; 1858-1861*; Canastota Publishing Co, Canastota NY: 2011.

Bailey, Goddard; *California -- Arrival of the Overland Mail -- Itinerary of the Route*; as reported by newspaper article; *New York Times* (NY) - October 14, 1858.

Bailey, Goddard; *Report to Postmaster General A.V. Brown - Full itinerary as reported by De Bow's Review and Industrial Resources, Statistics etc.;* published by *De Bow's Review*; New Orleans and Washington City; 1858. See specifically *Internal Improvements - 1. Wagon Road to the Pacific*; pp. 719-721.

Internet accessible at
http://books.google.com/books?id=5CYoAAAAYAAJ&pg=PA720&lpg=PA720&
dq=Cienega+de+los+Pimas&source=bl&ots=_5lZw_Bq23&sig=T6scCb8cpbY7K
wjxpYoNvZpcgvI&hl=en&ei=i6KnS6KNOIr2M5yprIED&sa=X&oi=book_result&
ct=result&resnum=2&ved=0CAwQ6AEwAQ#v=onepage&q=Cienega%20de%20
los%20Pimas&f=false (accessed March 22, 2010).

Conkling, Roscoe P. and Margaret B.; *The Butterfield Overland Mail, 1857–1869* (3 vols.); Glendale, CA: A. H. Clark Company, 1947.

Earthpoint; *Township and Range, Public Land Survey System on Google Earth*; internet data conversion system accessible at http://www.earthpoint.us/townships.aspx (accessed April 22, 2010).

Granger, Byrd Howell; *Arizona's Names - X Marks the Place, Historical Names of Places in Arizona;* Falconer Publishing Company, 1983.

Oregon - California Trails Association; *Learn. Connect. Preserve.*; Internet publication accessible at http://www.octa-trails.org/ (accessed October 9, 2010).

Ormsby, Waterman L.; *The Butterfield Overland Mail (Only Through Passenger on the First Westbound Stage)*; original publications *New York Herald* (NY) Sep 26 - Nov 19, 1858; republished by Henry E. Huntington Library and Art Gallery, San Marino CA, 1942 – 1998.

Talbot, Dan; *Historical Guide to the Mormon Battalion and Butterfield Trail;* Westernlore Press, 1992.

Cienega Creek Crossing to Tucson

April 21, 2011

Cienega Creek Crossing - near Vail, AZ • Pima County (N32° 01' 08.03", W110° 38' 46.48")

TO Presidio San Augustin - Tucson, AZ • Pima County (N32° 13' 23.80", W110° 58' 27.61")

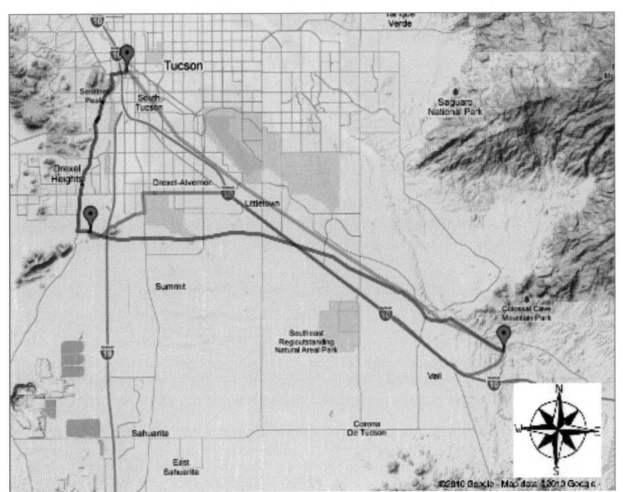

Approximate Actual Route, Cienega Springs to Tucson

33.5 miles (1858 Bailey itinerary = 35 miles)

Secondary Landmarks:

Mission San Xavier del Bac - approximate coordinates N32° 6' 24.08", W111° 0' 28.24"

Notes:

There is an important intermediate point to be considered along the route from Cienega Creek to Tucson -- said location being the Mission San Xavier del Bac, approximately 10 miles to the south and slightly west of the main Tucson Station.

The initial Butterfield route through this area substantially followed the earlier Mormon Battalion route but may have taken a slight divergence west to San Xavier del Bac and then north into Tucson. A more direct route bypassing San Xavier was later completed, however, and that shorter route was used during most of the Butterield period and thereafter.

Ahnert's 1973 and Talbot's 1992 route maps of the Butterfield Route bypass Mission San Xavier del Bac to the east. As Ahnert puts it "From the Cienega Springs Station the Butterfield Trail went through the old Vail ranch and passed through the present Davis - Monthan Air Force Base. The old road entered Tucson from the east over present 14th Street and then curved northwest from the corner of 14th Street and Scott Street to Main Street and then to the site of the old stage station."

Talbot clearly overlays the Butterfield and Mormon Battalion Routes through this segment -- bypassing San Xavier del Bac to the east of what is now the I-10 corridor.

The Oregon - California Trails Association (OCTA) has also done a significant amount of field research and mapping of this segment. That data; supplied by Chris Wray of OCTA as of October 28, 2010; has also been taken into account. Their detailed mapping data also bypasses San Xavier del Bac.

All of those routings, however fall about 11 miles shy of Bailey's 35 mile measure -- which 11 miles fall perfectly into line when the route is estimated via San Xavier del Bac.

In correspondence dated October 22, 2010, Ahnert noted "... [you are correct] about Bailey's 35 mile distance to Tucson from Seneca - Cienega Stage Station. For a short time the line went to [San Xavier del Bac] ..." and cites later writings to that effect by Silas St. John, an Arizona coachman during the Butterfield period.

• Data update as of March 2013 • It now appears that Butterfield adjusted to the shorter route at some point. In his 2011 study, Ahnert makes note of the probable two routes. Researcher Fred Yeck, based on the Conklings earlier data also identifies the shorter route. Here again, we have two legitimate routes that can be identified with Butterfield.

ˋThe first established settlement in the vicinity of Tucson dates to about 1699 when Father Francisco Kino established Mission San Xavier del Bac. A small settlement grew around the Mission after it was established and continued to thrive into and beyond the Butterfield period.

While the Mission San Xavier del Bac is not listed by either Ormsby or Bailey as an official Butterfield Station, it is likely that this historically important settlement would have been a "flag stop" with the coaches paying call at the mission if there were mail or passengers to be picked up or dropped off on a given trip.

Being one of the oldest settlements in a sparsely populated Arizona Territory, it is highly unlikely that the Butterfield would have completely by-passed the settlement at Mission San Xavier del Bac on the way to a smaller settlement at Tucson.

Mission San Xavier is listed on the National Register of Historic Places (1966 - #66000191). It is located at 1950 W San Xavier Road in modern Tucson (approximate coordinates N32° 6' 24.08", W111° 0' 28.24").

As to Tucson proper, Ormsby writes "Tucson is a small place, consisting of a few adobe houses. The inhabitants are mainly Mexicans. There are but few Americans, though they keep the two or three stores and are elected to the town offices. The town has considerably improved since the acquisition of the Territory by the United States."

According to a brief history from the City of Tucson, "In 1775, Hugo O'Conor establishes the Tucson Presidio. This year marks the official birthdate of the City of Tucson. Tucson becomes part of Mexico when it fights for independence in 1821. After the Gadsden Purchase in 1854, Tucson falls under the jurisdiction of the United States."

The Presidio and its Plaza were built in a square that is now in downtown Tucson and bounded by Church, Washington, Main and Pennington streets.

In 1867, this settlement around the Presidio was designated as the capital of the Arizona Territory.

In 2002, archaeological excavations were done by The Center for Desert Archaeology to design the Tucson Origins Heritage Park. A brief on that project notes "The archaeologists were surprised to find the deposits from the Presidio remarkably intact, just one inch below the asphalt of a parking lot north of the Transamerica building."

The Mission San Augustin and Presidio area is listed on the National Register of Historic Places (1979 - #79003808). Additional information is also available from the Tucson Presidio Trust for Historic Preservation; P.O. Box 1334, Tucson, Arizona 85702-1334 (Internet website can be accessed at http://www.tucsonpresidiotrust.org/).

Talbot indicates the Butterfield Station as having fronted on the south side of Alameda Street immediately west of the Presidio (south and a few feet west from the modern "T" intersection with N. Main Avenue).

Further, says Talbot, "Tucson was the last station in the [Overland Mail Company's] Sixth Division, traveling west. This division was under the supervision of William Buckley ... Tucson was a timetable station having three adobe buildings. The westbound mail was to arrive on Tuesdays and Fridays at 1:30 p.m., and the eastbound mail was due on Wednesdays and Saturdays at 3:00 a.m. The first westbound mail arrived at Tucson (on) Saturday, October 2, 1858, at 8:30 p.m., thirty-one hours delayed. The stationkeeper at Tucson was Samuel Hughes."

Ahnert places the Tucson Station "... almost directly across the street from the present City Hall in Tucson" and maps it at the intersection of Main Avenue at Alameda Street.

Tucson station can be placed in the vicinity of coordinates N32° 13' 23.80", W110° 58' 27.61". In correspondence dated October 22, 2010, Ahnert confirmed these coordinates according to his most recent measurement.

The Wray / OCTA mapping clearly follows the Ahnert (1973) and Talbot routes but does not specify coordinates for the Tucson Butterfield Station.

References:

Ahnert, Gerald T.; *Retracing the Butterfield Overland Trail through Arizona; a Guide to the Route of 1857-1861;* Westernlore Press; Tucson AZ; 1973 and *The Butterfield Trail and Overland Mail Company in Arizona; 1858-1861*; Canastota Publishing Co, Canastota NY: 2011.

Bailey, Goddard; *California -- Arrival of the Overland Mail -- Itinerary of the Route*; as reported by newspaper article; *New York Times* (NY) - October 14, 1858.

Bailey, Goddard; *Report to Postmaster General A.V. Brown - Full itinerary as reported by De Bow's Review and Industrial Resources, Statistics etc.;* published by *De Bow's Review*; New Orleans and Washington City; 1858. See specifically *Internal Improvements - 1. Wagon Road to the Pacific*; pp. 719-721. Internet accessible at http://books.google.com/books?id=5CYoAAAAYAAJ&pg=PA720&lpg=PA720& dq=Cienega+de+los+Pimas&source=bl&ots=_5lZw_Bq23&sig=T6scCb8cpbY7K wjxpYoNvZpcgvI&hl=en&ei=i6KnS6KNOIr2M5yprIED&sa=X&oi=book_result& ct=result&resnum=2&ved=0CAwQ6AEwAQ#v=onepage&q=Cienega%20de%20 los%20Pimas&f=false (accessed March 22, 2010).

Conkling, Roscoe P. and Margaret B.; *The Butterfield Overland Mail, 1857–1869* (3 vols.); Glendale, CA: A. H. Clark Company, 1947.

Earthpoint; *Township and Range, Public Land Survey System on Google Earth*; internet data conversion system accessible at http://www.earthpoint.us/townships.aspx (accessed April 22, 2010).

Oregon - California Trails Association; *Learn. Connect. Preserve.*; Internet publication accessible at http://www.octa-trails.org/ (accessed October 9, 2010).

Ormsby, Waterman L.; *The Butterfield Overland Mail (Only Through Passenger on the First Westbound Stage)*; original publications *New York Herald* (NY) Sep 26 - Nov 19, 1858; republished by Henry E. Huntington Library and Art Gallery, San Marino CA, 1942 – 1998.

Talbot, Dan; *Historical Guide to the Mormon Battalion and Butterfield Trail;* Westernlore Press, 1992.

Tucson (AZ), City of; *A Brief History of Tucson*; Internet publication accessible at http://cms3.tucsonaz.gov/history/tucson_history (accessed July 22, 2010).

Tucson to Picacho Pass

April 22, 2011

Presidio San Augustin – Tucson AZ • Pima County (N32° 13' 23.80", W110° 58' 27.61")

TO Picacho Peak State Park • Pinal County (N32° 38' 46.75", W111° 24' 0.18")

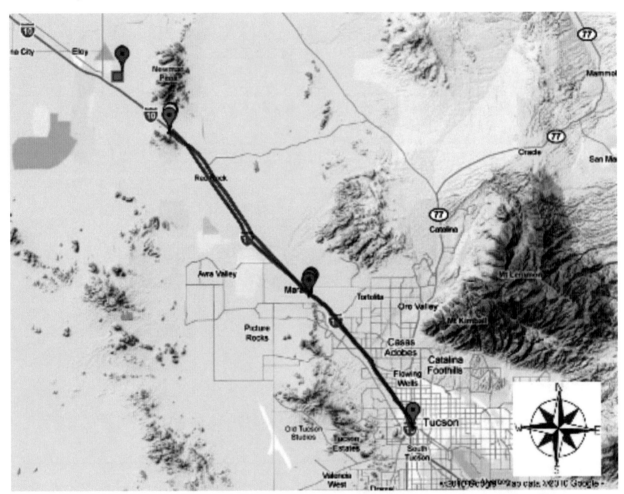

Approximate Actual Route, Tucson to Picacho Pass 36.75 miles

(17 miles Tucson to Pointer; 21.75 miles Pointer to

Picacho Pass) (1858 Bailey itinerary = 37 miles - 15

miles to Pointer Mountain / 22 miles to Picacho Peak)

Secondary Landmarks:

Pointer Mountain - approximate coordinates N32° 24' 54.21", W111° 09' 13.56"

Picacho Pass Station per Talbot - approximate coordinates N32° 44' 3.96", W111° 28' 52.74"

Mormon Trail Historical Marker - approximate coordinates N32° 39' 7.33", W111° 23' 54.15"

Notes:

The ongoing Butterfield Route is relatively easy to track as it follows the Mormon Battalion Route of 1846 and roughly tracks the Interstate 10 corridor of today.

In historical context, this is also the road improved by Col. James B. Leach (1857) and used by the San Antonio - San Diego Stages established by Skillman, Wasson, Birch et al. (1857). Leach's San Antonio - San Diego road appears the be what Postmaster General A.V. Brown referred to as "...the new road being opened and constructed under the direction of the Secretary of the Interior, [from El Paso TX] to Fort Yuma, California" in his 1857 general outline for the establishment of the Overland Mail Route.

In modern terms, Talbot and Ahnert (1973) include detailed maps of the immediate Tucson to Picacho Pass route. Because they compare so closely to one another, those maps clearly indicate a direct northwesterly route roughly tracking the later Southern Pacific Railroad tracks along and to the northeast of modern Interstate 10.

The Oregon - California Trails Association (OCTA) has also done a significant amount of field research and mapping of this segment. That data; supplied by Chris Wray of OCTA as of October 28, 2010; has also been taken into account. The detailed Wray / OCTA mapping data clearly indicates the northwesterly route as outlined in this segment map and concurs with the route reflected by Ahnert and Talbot.

There are several intermediate locations that help identify the Butterfield Route from Tucson to Picacho Pass.

The first of these intermediate points is Pointer Mountain (also referred to as "Point of Mountain" by some resources) at approximate coordinates N32° 24' 54.21", W111° 09' 13.56".

Ormsby speaks of the passage from Tucson to Picacho Pass as being 40 miles, but does not refer specifically to Pointer Mountain. Bailey, however, includes Pointer Mountain as a mileage point some 15 miles from the station at Tucson.

Of the route from Tucson to Pointer Mountain, Ahnert notes "The Butterfield Trail ... followed the approximate route that the present Southern Pacific Railroad takes northwest out of Tucson. The Butterfield Trail then followed along the Santa Cruz Wash north to Pointer Mountain Station, about 18 miles from the Tucson Station."

Neither Ahnert (1973) nor Talbot identify a Township and Range notation for Pointer Mountain. Talbot places it "at the Rillito railroad siding" near Marana. Ahnert's 1973 maps appear to place the Pointer Mountain Station to the east of Rillito along the main railroad tracks.

The Wray / OCTA mapping data notes Pointer Mountain as "Rillito Station" at coordinates N32° 25' 06.94", W111° 08' 52.86" -- slightly east of the report coordinates and Ahnert's 1973 location.

In correspondence dated October 22, 2010, however, Ahnert states that further research indicates the Pointer Mountain Station may have been on what is now private property approximately 2.5 miles north of the report coordinates (N32° 24' 54.21", W111° 09' 13.56").

Talbot does not speak of any ruins at Pointer Mountain as of 1992. He does seem rather specific about the probable layout of the station property, writing "The enclosing walls were sixty-five feet long by twenty-four feet long, with six rooms inside. The structure was built of adobe and a well was dug near the northwest corner. South of the main station building stood four smaller houses and probably a protecting wall around the station and neighboring buildings."

Ahnert also notes as of 1973 that "Little is known of the history of this station other than it was constructed of adobe. ... The site is in a plowed field and nothing is left of the old station."

Given lack of specific documentation and known ruins of the station at Pointer Mountain / Rillito, it may be that only a "ballpark" estimate of the station location can be made.

• Data Update as of March 2013 • Butterfield researcher Fred Yeck lives within approximately 3500 feet of the former Pointer Mountain Station and reports that it has been positively identified and is now recognized and preserved within the Los Morteros Conservancy Area. His coordinates for the site concur with those of Gerald Ahnert in his 2011 publication at coordinates N32° 23' 22.92", W111° 8' 10.68".

The second and third notable intermediate points along the route are adjacent to one another. The first of those is an Arizona Historical Marker identifying the route of the Mormon Battalion, located at approximate coordinates N32° 39' 7.33", W111° 23' 54.15". That marker is slightly northeast of the entrance to Picacho Peak State Park (approximate coordinates N32° 38' 46.75", W111° 24' 0.18").

Picacho Pass has been definitively identified as a stop for the earlier Mormon Battalion that was also used by the Butterfield coaches. The Mormon Battalion made camp at Picacho Pass on December 17th, 1846.

The pass is also famous as having been the site of the westernmost battle of the Civil War. That skirmish, the "Battle of Picacho Pass", took place on April 15th, 1862. The battle pitted a Union Army of 1,400 troops under the command of Brigadier General James H. Carleton against an outnumbered contingent of Confederates commanded by Captain Sherrod Hunter who had occupied Tucson on February 28th, 1862.

The Confederates ambushed the Union troops as they entered the pass; however, the sheer number of the Union Army overpowered the Confederates. Having evacuated Tucson, Hunter was then forced to withdraw from Picacho Pass as well. Thereupon, Hunter's Confederates attempted a retreat to the nearest Confederate strongholds along the Rio Grande near Santa Fe and El Paso, taking several Union prisoners with them. That retreat is well-documented and tragic, as Apaches based in the Chiricahua Mountains attacked Hunter's troops many times along the retreat. As the retreat to Fort Yuma became a running fight for survival against the Apaches, the Confederates armed their Union prisoners and the former foes fought side by side to defend themselves from Apache attacks. The ragged Confederates and their prisoners arrived at the Rio Grande encampments on May 27, 1862. The short-lived occupation of the Arizona Territory, the westernmost territory held by the Confederacy, had ended.

Picacho Pass is listed on the National Register of Historic Places (Picacho Pass Skirmish Site / Overland Mail Company Stage Station at Picacho Pass; 2002 - #02001384).

For the purposes of this report, we have identified the approximate location of the Picacho Peak / Picacho Pass station within Picacho Peak State park near the southeastern mouth of the pass although the station site may have been slightly northeast of the park property.

Ahnert (1973) notes that the Butterfield route through this area " ...followed McClellan Wash to a point near present day Picacho. As in many areas where the stageline followed the washes, there is evidence that the trail paralleled the wash or was in the wash, depending on whether or not water was present." He also notes that "There are no ruins left to mark the exact site, but the present Southern Pacific tracks ether pass directly over the site of the old station or very close to it."

While Ahnert (1973) does not specify an exact geographical placement, his description and mapping would appear to place the station site along the railroad tracks just east of the Mormon Trail Historical Marker previously mentioned at approximate coordinates N32° 38' 46.75", W111° 24' 0.18". In correspondence dated October 22, 2010, Ahnert confirmed placement of the station site at these coordinates.

•Data update as of March 2013 • With publication of his revised study, Ahnert reconfirmed this location with specific latitude and longitude coordinates at N32° 39' 16.20", W111° 23' 46.32".

The Wray / OCTA mapping data places the Picacho Station at coordinates N32° 38' 59.95", W111° 23' 29.89", slightly east of the report coordinates and southeast of the Mormon Trail Historical Marker / Ahnert 1973 location description.

Talbot places the Picacho Pass / Picacho Peak station some 10 miles beyond the entrance to Picacho Peak State Park – which site, however, appears to be a post-Butterfield Station location mistakenly identified as the Butterield site. He cites the location as being at the northeast corner of Township 8S, Range 8E, Section 14. Specifically, Talbot's location would place the Picacho Peak / Picacho Pass station in the vicinity of coordinates N32° 44' 3.96", W111° 28' 52.74" near Eloy AZ -- a point at which the Butterfield Route and the Mormon Battalion Route directly intersects the earlier de Anza route (1775-1776). That placement, however, is well beyond the mileage measurement noted by Bailey.

In correspondence dated October 22, 2010, however, Ahnert states that the Talbot location "was not a Butterfield Station, but one from the 1870s".

The Wray / OCTA mapping data also recognizes Talbot's Eloy-area location as a latter-1800s station site.

References:

Ahnert, Gerald T.; *Retracing the Butterfield Overland Trail through Arizona; a Guide to the Route of 1857-1861;* Westernlore Press; Tucson AZ; 1973 and *The Butterfield Trail and Overland Mail Company in Arizona; 1858-1861*; Canastota Publishing Co, Canastota NY: 2011.

Bailey, Goddard; *California -- Arrival of the Overland Mail -- Itinerary of the Route*; as reported by newspaper article; *New York Times* (NY) - October 14, 1858.

Bailey, Goddard; *Report to Postmaster General A.V. Brown - Full itinerary as reported by De Bow's Review and Industrial Resources, Statistics etc.;* published by *De Bow's Review*; New Orleans and Washington City; 1858. See specifically *Internal Improvements - 1. Wagon Road to the Pacific*; pp. 719-721. Internet accessible at http://books.google.com/books?id=5CYoAAAAYAAJ&pg=PA720&lpg=PA720&dq=Cienega+de+los+Pimas&source=bl&ots=_5lZw_Bq23&sig=T6scCb8cpbY7KwjxpYoNvZpcgvI&hl=en&ei=i6KnS6KNOIr2M5yprIED&sa=X&oi=book_result&ct=result&resnum=2&ved=0CAwQ6AEwAQ#v=onepage&q=Cienega%20de%20los%20Pimas&f=false (accessed March 22, 2010).

Conkling, Roscoe P. and Margaret B.; *The Butterfield Overland Mail, 1857–1869* (3 vols.); Glendale, CA: A. H. Clark Company, 1947.

Earthpoint; *Township and Range, Public Land Survey System on Google Earth*; internet data conversion system accessible at http://www.earthpoint.us/townships.aspx (accessed April 22, 2010).

National Park Service; *Juan Bautista de Anza National Historic Trail Guide Pinal County)*; Internet publication available at http://www.solideas.com/DeAnza/TrailGuide/ (accessed July 28, 2010).

National Register of Historic Places; *National Register Locations by State*; Internet publication; accessible at

http://www.nationalregisterofhistoricplaces.com/state.html (accessed May 3, 2010).

Oregon - California Trails Association; *Learn. Connect. Preserve.*; Internet publication accessible at http://www.octa-trails.org/ (accessed October 9, 2010).

Ormsby, Waterman L.; *The Butterfield Overland Mail (Only Through Passenger on the First Westbound Stage)*; original publications *New York Herald* (NY) Sep 26 - Nov 19, 1858; republished by Henry E. Huntington Library and Art Gallery, San Marino CA, 1942 – 1998.

Talbot, Dan; *Historical Guide to the Mormon Battalion and Butterfield Trail;* Westernlore Press, 1992.

View of Picacho Peak from Picacho Pass Station site (N32.649, W111.392).
Photo by Fred Yeck (2011).

Picacho Pass to Sacaton

April 22, 2011

Picacho Peak State Park • Pinal County (N32° 38' 46.75", W111° 24' 0.18")

TO Sacaton, AZ • Pinal County (N33° 4' 51.64", W111° 44' 40.49")

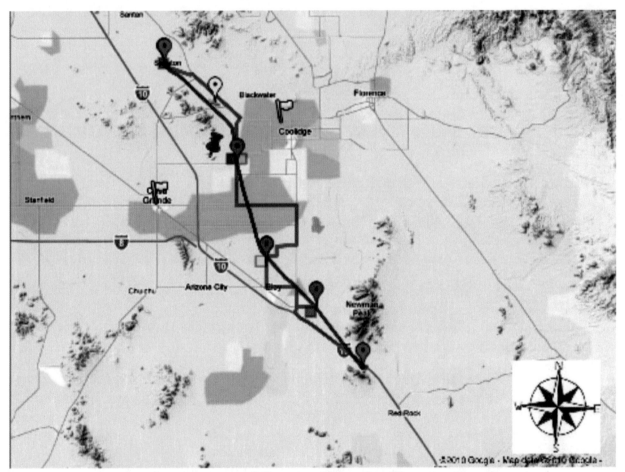

Approximate Actual Route, Picacho Pass to Sacaton

37.6 miles (1858 Bailey itinerary = 37 miles)

Secondary Landmarks:

Picacho Pass per Talbot - approximate coordinates N32° 44' 3.96", W111° 28' 52.74"

Blue Water Station per Talbot - approximate coordinates N32° 47' 57.91", W111° 34' 34.81"

Oneida Station per Talbot and Ahnert - approximate coordinates N32° 56' 17.66", W111° 37' 6.94"

Thin Mountain per Talbot - approximate coordinates N33° 1' 30.21", W111° 39' 26.47"

Notes:

As a region, this next segment enters what has been referred to historically as the "Pima Villages" area. Dating back to the Mormon Battalion movement in the 1840s and earlier, the area was known for several small permanent and semi-permanent Indian settlements.

The Butterfield Route through this segment follows a well-known historical corridor that can be traced to the route of Spanish explorer Juan Bautista de Anza (1775-1776); the Mormon Battalion (1846-1847); the road established by Col. James B. Leach (1857); and the course of the San Antonio - San Diego Stage route established by Skillman, Wasson, Birch et al. (1857).

In modern context, Ahnert (1973 and 2011) and Talbot (1992) include detailed maps of the Picacho to Sacaton Butterfield Route. Given close comparison to one another, those maps clearly indicate the northwesterly route as indicated in this report.

The Oregon - California Trails Association (OCTA) has also done a significant amount of field research and mapping of this segment. That data; supplied by Chris Wray of OCTA as of October 28, 2010; has also been taken into account.

The detailed Wray / OCTA mapping data clearly indicates the due northwesterly route as outlined in this segment map and concurs with the route reflected by Ahnert and Talbot. There are three intermediate Butterfield-related landmarks along this route segment. None of these locations are listed by either Ormsby or Bailey in their itineraries of the first westward and eastward trips on the Butterfield, however. Both of those itineraries indicate a nonstop trip between Picacho Pass and Sacaton.

The "Blue Water Station" has been placed fairly reliably. Talbot reports that the Blue Water Station was "one of the intermediate change and water stations that were established in the later part of 1858 and 1859."

Of the station specifically, Talbot writes, "It had a well that supplied plenty of water for the station even in the dry season". He indicates that Blue Water Station was located "about three miles west of Toltec" and notes that "Today the site, in a cultivated field, has no remains to indicate the size or extent of the old station." By particulars, Talbot places Blue Water within Township 7S, Range 7E, Section 24. This location would place the station at approximately N32° 47' 57.91", W111° 34' 34.81".

Talbot's 1992 Township and Range location for the Blue Water Station mirrors Ahnert's placement as of 1973. Ahnert also notes that "Today there are no ruins left to mark the exact site. The site is now in a cultivated field."

In correspondence dated October 22, 2010, Ahnert notes that the report coordinates (N32° 47' 57.91", W111° 34' 34.81") are within 2600 feet of his most recent coordinate measurement. • Data update as of March 2013 • With publication of his 2011 study, Ahnert placed the specific coordinates for the Blue Water Station at N32° 49' 18.48", W111° 32' 21.84". Fred Yeck's findings are in concurrence with Ahnert.

The Wray / OCTA mapping data concurs with the Blue Water Station coordinates, placing it at specific coordinates N32° 47' 59.90", W111° 34' 04.61".

Talbot also writes that the route from Blue Water to Sacaton "... headed north along the east side of the Sacaton Mountains, then westward through the gap between them and Thin Mountain." This approximate placement for the Blue Water Station follows a route from Picacho to Sacaton that would be in line with his description of a route moving to the east of the Sacaton Mountains.

A second station site listed by Talbot is referred to as "Oneida Station." Information about this location is rather sparse, however.

Talbot (1992) notes that the Oneida Station "was built of adobe in late 1858 or early 1859." He cites the location as being in the vicinity of Township 5S, Range 7E, Section 35. Ahnert (1973) places the Oneida Station slightly to the west of Talbot's within Township 5S, Range 7E, Section 34.

Comparing the Talbot and Ahnert township and range placements to Ahnert's mapped location, which is directly southwest of Black Butte, would appear to place the Oneida Station on the southern verge of Sections 34 and 35 -- in the vicinity of W McCartney Road and N Signal Peak Road. Approximate coordinates for that intersection are N32° 56' 17.66", W111° 37' 6.94".

In correspondence dated October 22, 2010, Ahnert noted that the Oneida Station coordinates at N32° 56' 17.66", W111° 37' 6.94" are within 3000 feet of his most recent coordinate measurement.

• Data update as of March 2013 • In his 2011 publication, Ahnert cited specific coordinates for the Oneida Station at N32° 56' 36.60", W111° 36' 34.20". Yeck's research confirms those coordinates.

The Wray / OCTA mapping data places Oneida Station at coordinates N32° 56' 32.47", W111° 36' 38.67" -- slightly northeast of the report coordinates and within bounds of Talbot's citation of Township 5S, Range 7E, Section 34.

Oneida Station appears to be contiguous to the boundaries of Casa Grande National Monument, administered by the National Park Service. It is possible that additional consultation with personnel at Casa Grande National Monument might lend more light to the exact location of the Oneida Station and additional interpretive data.

The next stop listed by Ormsby and Bailey presents us with a slight variant in the location's spelling, being referred to as "Sacatoon" in those contemporaneous reports. The same community can, however, be located on modern maps as "Sacaton."

Talbot notes that the further track of the Butterfield route to Sacaton continued "to the south of Thin Mountain," a geographical feature that can be identified at coordinates N33° 1' 30.21", W111° 39' 26.47" between Coolidge and Sacaton.

• Data update as of March 2013 • Ahnert 2011 reports the discovery of several old wagon ruts etween Oneida Station and Sacaton that essentially reinforce the presence of the original route depicted in this report with only minor deviations.

Sacaton was a Pima Indian settlement that was tolerant of or friendly to Euro-American travelers and emigrants. The Butterfield Station at Sacaton was constructed in 1858 and operated by stationmaster Hiram Stevens.

Talbot places the location of the Sacaton Station about 0.1 mile northeast of the report coordinates "at the center of Township 4S, Range 6E, Section 16 (approximate coordinates N33° 4' 53.12", W111° 44' 46.78").

Ahnert's 1973 narrative is somewhat unclear regarding the site of the Sacaton Station. His mapping appears to place the site in general accord with Talbot and the coordinates cited in this report. In correspondence dated October 22, 2010, however, Ahnert indicates the actual Sacaton Station site may have been toward the northwestern corner of Township 4S, Range 6E, Section 16 -- approximately 0.5 miles northwest of report coordinates N33° 4' 53.12", W111° 44' 46.78".

The Wray / OCTA mapping data also identifies both of the sites as possible Sacaton Station locations but does not specify a single identified site.

• Data update as of March 2013 • Ahnert 2011 places specific coordinates for the Sacaton Station at N33° 4' 21.72", W111° 43' 14.52". Yeck's research confirms that location. That location is approximately two miles east of the report coordinates. It is clear that actual location of the Sacaton Station remains in doubt ad requires additional scrutiny and study.

References:

Ahnert, Gerald T.; *Retracing the Butterfield Overland Trail through Arizona; a Guide to the Route of 1857-1861;* Westernlore Press; Tucson AZ; 1973 and *The Butterfield Trail and Overland Mail Company in Arizona; 1858-1861*; Canastota Publishing Co, Canastota NY: 2011.

Bailey, Goddard; *California -- Arrival of the Overland Mail -- Itinerary of the Route*; as reported by newspaper article; *New York Times* (NY) - October 14, 1858.

Bailey, Goddard; *Report to Postmaster General A.V. Brown - Full itinerary as reported by De Bow's Review and Industrial Resources, Statistics etc.;* published by *De Bow's Review*; New Orleans and Washington City; 1858. See specifically *Internal Improvements - 1. Wagon Road to the Pacific*; pp. 719-721. Internet accessible at http://books.google.com/books?id=5CYoAAAAYAAJ&pg=PA720&lpg=PA720&dq=Cienega+de+los+Pimas&source=bl&ots=_5lZw_Bq23&sig=T6scCb8cpbY7KwjxpYoNvZpcgvI&hl=en&ei=i6KnS6KNOIr2M5yprIED&sa=X&oi=book_result&ct=result&resnum=2&ved=0CAwQ6AEwAQ#v=onepage&q=Cienega%20de%20los%20Pimas&f=false (accessed March 22, 2010).

Conkling, Roscoe P. and Margaret B.; *The Butterfield Overland Mail, 1857–1869* (3 vols.); Glendale, CA: A. H. Clark Company, 1947.

Earthpoint; *Township and Range, Public Land Survey System on Google Earth*; internet data conversion system accessible at http://www.earthpoint.us/townships.aspx (accessed April 22, 2010).

National Park Service; *Juan Bautista de Anza National Historic Trail Guide (Pima and Pinal Counties)*; Internet publication available at http://www.solideas.com/DeAnza/TrailGuide/ (accessed July 28, 2010).

Oregon - California Trails Association; *Learn. Connect. Preserve.*; Internet publication accessible at http://www.octa-trails.org/ (accessed October 9, 2010).

Ormsby, Waterman L.; *The Butterfield Overland Mail (Only Through Passenger on the First Westbound Stage)*; original publications *New York Herald* (NY) Sep 26 - Nov 19, 1858; republished by Henry E. Huntington Library and Art Gallery, San Marino CA, 1942 – 1998.

Talbot, Dan; *Historical Guide to the Mormon Battalion and Butterfield Trail;* Westernlore Press, 1992.

**Vicinity of Sacaton Station, Sacaton AZ (N33.070, W111.720).
Photo by Fred Yeck (2011).**

Sacaton to Maricopa Wells

April 22, 2011

Sacaton, AZ • Pinal County (N33° 4' 51.64", W111° 44' 40.49")

TO Maricopa Wells - Maricopa, AZ • Pinal County (N33° 09' 43.18", W112° 05' 02.52")

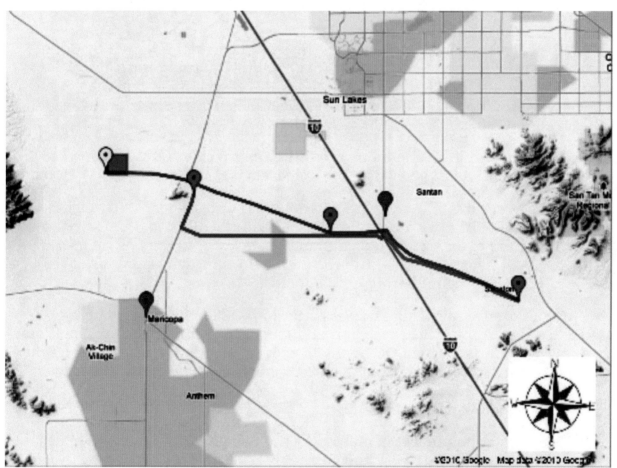

Approximate Actual Route, Sacaton to Maricopa Wells

22.25 miles (1858 Bailey itinerary = 22 miles)

Secondary Landmarks:

Sweetwater - landmark only per Talbot - modern coordinates N33° 7' 54.98", W111° 50' 24.00"

Casa Blanca per Talbot - modern coordinates N33° 7' 10.60", W111° 53' 17.67"

Notes:

The ongoing segment to Maricopa Wells can be fairly readily identified, although it is important that the endpoint at Maricopa Wells not be mistaken for the modern city of Maricopa.

This segment continues along the historical corridor followed by Spanish explorer Juan Bautista de Anza (1775-1776); the Mormon Battalion (1846-1847); the road established by Col. James B. Leach (1857); and the course of the San Antonio - San Diego Stage route established by Skillman, Wasson, Birch et al. (1857).

Ormsby specifically mentions the route from Sacaton to Maricopa as being 24 miles, while Bailey lists the mileage as 22 miles.

In modern context, Ahnert (1973 and 2011) and Talbot (1992) include detailed maps of the Sacaton to Maricopa Butterfield Route. Compared to one another, those maps clearly indicate the northwesterly route as indicated in this report. Talbot maps the Butterfield and Mormon Battalion routes as being one and the same through this area.

The Oregon - California Trails Association (OCTA) has also done a significant amount of field research and mapping of this segment. That data; supplied by Chris Wray of OCTA as of October 28, 2010; has also been taken into account. The detailed Wray / OCTA mapping data clearly indicates a northwesterly route as outlined in this segment map and concurs with the route reflected by Ahnert and Talbot.

Talbot mentions that "Six miles past the Sacaton Station the road passed by an old Indian trading post known as Sweetwater. This is believed to have been the location of Fort Barrett, established May 1862 by the California Volunteers and named in honor of Lt. Barrett, who was killed in the Battle of Picacho Pass." He does not, however, offer a specific location for either Sweetwater or Fort Barrett.

There is also an intermediate station on this leg that can be located to good approximation, although it was not mentioned by either Ormsby or

Bailey. Known as the Casa Blanca Station, it was located in the vicinity of the present town of Casa Blanca (N33° 7' 10.60", W111° 53' 17.67"). Station keeper Ammi White built the station here in 1858 and later operated the first steam powered flour mill in the region at his station.

Talbot identifies Casa Blanca Station as having been "about 11 miles northwest of Sacaton Station near the present Indian Village of Casa Blanca." Breaking with his usual methodology, Talbot does not specify township, range and section quadrants for Sweetwater, Casa Blanca Station or Maricopa Wells.

Neither does Ahnert (1973) specify township and range for Casa Blanca. His mapping appears to concur approximately with the report coordinates (N33° 7' 10.60", W111° 53' 17.67"). In correspondence dated October 22, 2010, Ahnert noted that the report coordinates are within about 1.2 miles of his most recent coordinate measure. Ahnert maps the Casa Blanca Station just north of a small cemetery. Unfortunately, however, this cemetery cannot be located by present map work alone. It is likely that field research in Casa Blanca during the planning and implementation phases may be able to physically locate and GPS that cemetery.

The Wray / OCTA mapping data places the Casa Blanca Station at coordinates N33° 07' 15.56", W111° 54' 31.21" -- approximately 1.2 miles west of the report coordinates. The Wray coordinates appear to support the vicinity of Ahnert's description.

• Data update as of March 2013 • In his 2011 publication, Ahnert specified coordinates for the Casa Blanca Station at N33° 7' 24.60", W111° 54' 32.76" – which essentially concurs with the Wray / OCTA coordinates. Researcher Fred Yeck concurs with those coordinates.

The next site at Maricopa Wells was used as a water source and campground as far back as the Spanish explorations during the late seventeenth century. Originally called Santa Teresa, the Maricopa Wells were an extremely important spot to the history of Arizona. These wells were initially hand dug by the Mormon Battalion in 1846 as they prepared to cross the desert westward. The area became a major convergence of the main north-south and east-west trails through the territory.

The actual site of this station is difficult to access today. This is protected property located on an Indian reservation and requires special permission to visit. The nearest one can get on public roads is toward the east foot of Pima Butte. Maricopa Wells can be placed on modern maps at approximate coordinates N33 09' 43.18", W112 05' 02.52".

In correspondence dated October 12, 2010, Cheryl Blanchard (archaeologist for the Bureau of Land Management Lower Sonoran Field Office - Phoenix) noted that the Maricopa Wells site "... is located on the Gila River Indian Community (GRIC) lands and one needs to obtain special permission to go anywhere on the reservation."

Ahnert (1973) places Maricopa Wells slightly east of the modern coordinates within Township 3S, Range 3E, Section 17. In correspondence dated October 22, 2010, Ahnert stated that the report coordinates N33° 09' 43.18", W112° 05' 02.52" are within 1000 feet of his most recent coordinate measurement. • Data update as of March 2013 • Anert's 2011 publication states the Maricopa Wells coordinates as +33° 9' 41.04", -112° 4' 50.52", which is I lie with the report coordinates. Yeck concurs.

The Wray / OCTA mapping data places Maricopa Wells at coordinates N33° 09' 44.96", W112° 04' 44.03" -- very slightly east of the report coordinates and within Township 3S, Range 3E, Section 17 as reported by Ahnert (1973).

The present city of Maricopa AZ, southeast of the old wells, was established in the 1870s.

Information from the City of Maricopa (which celebrates "Stagecoach Days" annually) notes:

"A 1694 journal entry by Father Eusebio Francisco Kino records a description of what would become Maricopa Wells. He noted an established agricultural community populated by friendly Native Americans who were established traders.

In the mid-1800's, when everything south of the Gila River was still part of Mexico, Maricopa Wells was a dependable source of water along the Gila Trail. It became an important and famous stage stop for the Butterfield Overland Mail Line that stretched from Saint Louis to San Francisco.

The 1870's brought the railroad south of the wells and the ever-adaptable people of the area moved to meet the needs of progress. Phoenix was little more than a tiny village on the Salt River but growing political influence led to the building of a spur line from Maricopa to Phoenix. Today's Maricopa Road (John Wayne Parkway) lies over the top of that old rail line.

By the 1880s, local rancher E. O. Stratton would note in his memoirs "Though small, Maricopa Wells was a busy place. The stages passing twice a day, one eastbound and one westbound, changed animals and fed their passengers here. When troops were discharged - and this was often - the stages were full both ways. At other times there was a predominance of passengers from the west. Not only were many Californians coming into the country, but there also were the Easterners who had gone by train or around the Horn to San Francisco, then came down the coast to San Diego and into Arizona by stage. Then, too, Maricopa Wells was the division point for Phoenix, Fort McDowell on the Verde, and other places to the north. The camping ground outside the enclosure was also a busy place. Great freight trains of three or four wagons and eight to twenty mules were often camped there; and detachments of soldiers - from a few scouts to one or more companies - might turn in for the night. Soldiers scouting through the immediate country usually made Maricopa Wells their supply station; and all westbound traffic, whether or not they camped, had to load up with enough water to last across the desert from Maricopa to Gila Bend, a distance of forty-five miles which meant at least one night's camp."

References:

Ahnert, Gerald T.; *Retracing the Butterfield Overland Trail through Arizona; a Guide to the Route of 1857-1861;* Westernlore Press; Tucson AZ; 1973 and *The Butterfield Trail and Overland Mail Company in Arizona; 1858-1861*; Canastota Publishing Co, Canastota NY: 2011.

Bailey, Goddard; *California -- Arrival of the Overland Mail -- Itinerary of the Route*; as reported by newspaper article; *New York Times* (NY) - October 14, 1858.

Bailey, Goddard; *Report to Postmaster General A.V. Brown - Full itinerary as reported by De Bow's Review and Industrial Resources, Statistics etc.;* published by *De Bow's Review*; New Orleans and Washington City; 1858. See specifically *Internal Improvements - 1. Wagon Road to the Pacific*; pp. 719-721. Internet accessible at http://books.google.com/books?id=5CYoAAAAYAAJ&pg=PA720&lpg=PA720& dq=Cienega+de+los+Pimas&source=bl&ots=_5lZw_Bq23&sig=T6scCb8cpbY7K wjxpYoNvZpcgvI&hl=en&ei=i6KnS6KNOIr2M5yprIED&sa=X&oi=book_result& ct=result&resnum=2&ved=0CAwQ6AEwAQ#v=onepage&q=Cienega%20de%20 los%20Pimas&f=false (accessed March 22, 2010).

Barnes, Will C.; *Arizona Place Names*; University of Arizona Press; Tucson AZ; 1960.

Conkling, Roscoe P. and Margaret B.; *The Butterfield Overland Mail, 1857–1869* (3 vols.); Glendale, CA: A. H. Clark Company, 1947.

Earthpoint; *Township and Range, Public Land Survey System on Google Earth*; internet data conversion system accessible at http://www.earthpoint.us/townships.aspx (accessed April 22, 2010).

Maricopa AZ (City of); *Our History*; Internet publication accessible at http://www.maricopa-az.gov/vns/index.php/welcome-to-maricopa/our-history (accessed July 27, 2010).

National Park Service; *Juan Bautista de Anza National Historic Trail Guide (Pinal and Maricopa Counties)*; Internet publication available at http://www.solideas.com/DeAnza/TrailGuide/Pinal/index.html (accessed July 28, 2010).

Oregon - California Trails Association; *Learn. Connect. Preserve.*; Internet publication accessible at http://www.octa-trails.org/ (accessed October 9, 2010).

Ormsby, Waterman L.; *The Butterfield Overland Mail (Only Through Passenger on the First Westbound Stage)*; original publications *New York Herald* (NY) Sep 26 - Nov 19, 1858; republished by Henry E. Huntington Library and Art Gallery, San Marino CA, 1942 – 1998.

Talbot, Dan; *Historical Guide to the Mormon Battalion and Butterfield Trail;* Westernlore Press, 1992.

Maricopa Wells to Gila Ranch

April 22, 2011

Maricopa Wells - Maricopa, AZ • Pinal County (N33° 09' 43.18", W112° 05' 02.52")

TO Gila Ranch (approximate per Talbot) - Gila Bend, AZ • Maricopa County (N33° 0' 26.19", W112° 41' 29.61")

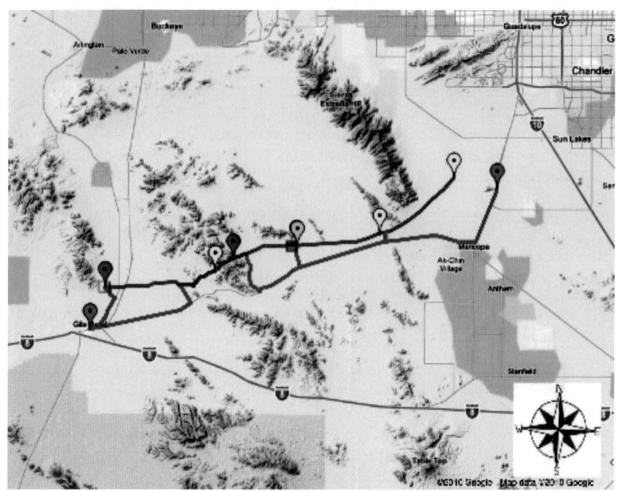

Approximate Actual Route, Maricopa Wells to Gila Ranch

39.5 miles (1858 Bailey itinerary = 40 miles)

Secondary Landmarks:

North Tank (Montezuma Head Tank) - approximate coordinates N33° 5' 1.42", W112° 12' 49.32"

Desert Station per Talbot - approximate coordinates N33° 3' 57.07", W112° 21' 30.54"

Butterfield Pass - approximate coordinates N33° 02' 49.16", W112° 28' 07.56"

South Tank - aka "Happy Camp Cistern"; aka "Forty-mile Desert Tank" - approximate coordinates N33° 1' 49.80", W112° 29' 58.20"

Notes:

The ongoing Butterfield Route continues along the historical corridor followed by Spanish explorer Juan Bautista de Anza (1775-1776); the Mormon Battalion (1846-1847); the road established by Col. James B. Leach (1857); and the course of the San Antonio - San Diego Stageline established by Skillman, Wasson, Birch et al. (1857).

In modern context, Ahnert (1973 and 2011) and Talbot (1992) include detailed maps of the Maricopa Wells to Gila Ranch Butterfield Route. Given the close comparison to one another, those maps clearly indicate a southwesterly to westerly route as indicated in this report.

Talbot maps the Butterfield and Mormon Battalion routes as being one and the same through this area.

The Oregon - California Trails Association (OCTA) has also done a significant amount of field research and mapping of this segment. That data, supplied by Chris Wray of OCTA as of October 28, 2010, has also been taken into account. The detailed Wray / OCTA mapping data clearly indicates the southwesterly to westerly route as outlined in this segment map and concurs with the route reflected by Ahnert and Talbot.

Historically, the traverse of the "Forty Mile Desert" section the Sonoran Desert in this area -- was infamous as a long, dry and perilous haul between Maricopa Wells and the next natural water at Gila Ranch. According to some sources, by late 1858 - early 1859 the Butterfield Overland company had built three additional water tanks along the route to help break the long dry haul -- referred to as North Tank, Desert Station and South Tank.

Those three tanks were reportedly constructed so that reliable sources of water were no farther apart than 10 miles through this arid landscape. Water to replenish those tanks was hauled by wagon from Maricopa Wells and Gila Ranch.

The original "North Tank" was reportedly located approximately 10 miles west / southwest of Maricopa Wells. While it is difficult to pinpoint the exact location of this purported "North Tank" from presently known sources, mileage references along the known route (10 miles from Maricopa Wells) would place it in the vicinity of coordinates N33° 5' 1.42", W112° 12' 49.32".

Neither Ahnert (1973) nor Talbot (1992) speak specifically to this North Tank site. Likewise, in correspondence dated October 12, 2010, Cheryl Blanchard (Bureau of Land Management Lower Sonoran Field Office - Phoenix), could not confirm a documented Butterfield site in this vicinity.

In correspondence dated October 22, 2010, however, Ahnert stated he had discovered indications of this location referred to in the writings of Silas St. John, coachman and Butterfield employee, who referred to the location as the "Montezuma Head Tank". Ahnert said he has visited the location on some preliminary studies and it was an above-ground tank. He reported that the Montezuma Head Tank is within 1.2 miles of the coordinates listed for the "North Tank" coordinates above.

• Data update as of March 2013 • In his 2011 publication, Ahnert states specifically that the North Tank / Montezuma Head Tank was located at coordinates N33° 04' 46", W112° 13' 49".

The Wray / OCTA data very specifically identifies the route passing through this vicinity as determined via field research and overlays of GLO maps from the 1870s to modern maps, but does not specifically identify a "North Tank" location.

The location of the intermediary "Desert Station / Desert Well Station" is more readily determined. Talbot places Desert Station as having been on the "east side" of Township 4S, Range 1W, Section 21.

Ahnert (1973) mentions the "Desert Well Station" but does not specify coordinates or Township, Range, Section data. He does locate the station "about 5.5 miles west of Mobile ... on Waterman Wash."

Waterman Wash is an easily identifiable topographic / geological landmark. It is a watercourse running essentially north-south through this area. Talbot places the Desert Station on the western edge of Waterman Wash, which location appears to concur with Ahnert's description.

Given those descriptions, Desert Station would have been in the vicinity of coordinates N33° 3' 57.07", W112° 21' 30.54".

Blanchard reported Desert Station to have been within triangular bounds cornered as follows:

NW perimeter - N33° 3' 57.165", W112° 21' 28.446"

NE perimeter - N33° 3' 56.866", W112° 21' 26.128"

SW perimeter - N33° 3' 54.227", W112° 21' 29.943".

The zone identified by Blanchard straddles Township 4S, Range 1W, Section 21 (the Desert Station section identified by Talbot) and the neighboring Township 4S, Range 1W, Section 22 to the east.

She identified a centroid for this zone at coordinates N33° 3' 56.2", W112° 21' 27.66". The location of the centroid point identified by Blanchard is approximately 260 feet southeast of the approximate Talbot and Ahnert site.

In correspondence dated October 22, 2010, Ahnert stated that the Desert Station site is within 3100 feet of coordinates N33° 3' 57.07", W112° 21' 30.54" according to his most recent location measurements.

• Data update as of March 2013 • In his 2011 publication, Ahnert states specifically that the Desert Station was located at coordinates N33° 03' 59", W112° 21' 38". Yeck concurs.

The Wray / OCTA mapping data clearly identifies Desert Wells Station at coordinates N33° 4' 00.40", W112° 21' 30.79" -- in concurrence with the report coordinates and Ahnert's most recent measurement.

Beyond Desert Station the Butterfield Route passed through what came to be called "Butterfield Pass." Butterfield Pass can be located on some commercial at approximate coordinates N33° 02' 49.16", W112° 28' 07.56".

Ahnert (1973 and 2011) mentions the Butterfield route in this segment as passing through "Pima Pass." In correspondence dated October 22, 2010, Ahnert confirmed that "Pima Pass" was the name commonly used for this spot during the Butterfield Period and that "Pima Pass" and "Butterfield Pass" are one and the same.

The Wray / OCTA mapping data clearly follows the course via Butterfield Pass / Pima Pass.

The "South Tank" was located approximately 10 miles east of Gila Ranch and is variously referred to in modern terms as "Happy Camp Cistern" and "Fortymile Desert Tank". This tank can be located on modern maps at approximate coordinates N33° 1' 49.80", W112° 29' 58.20".

Blanchard noted the "Happy Camp / Fortymile Tank" location as being in the vicinity of coordinates N33° 1' 43.388", W112° 29' 59.041".

Without providing a specific location, Ahnert (1973) mentions "Happy Camp." However, he states that the present cistern "... was built directly across the trail from the [original] tank after Butterfield Overland suspended operations." In correspondence dated October 22, 2010, Ahnert stated that coordinates N33° 1' 43.388", W112° 29' 59.041" are within 300 feet of his most recent location measurements for the South Tank (a.k.a. "Pima Pass Tank"). That location is also in close proximity to the site as identified by Blanchard.

The Wray / OCTA mapping data again clearly indicates the route through this vicinity but does not specifically cite a location for Happy Camp / Forty Mile Desert Tank / South Tank.

The Gila Ranch Station, by all accounts, was located near the hard bend of the Gila River on the eastern boundary of the present town of Gila Bend. It was a timetable station with the westbound stages due at 9:00 p.m. on Wednesdays and Saturdays; the eastbound stages were due at 7:30 p.m. on Mondays and Thursdays.

According to Talbot, the original adobe station was destroyed in an Indian raid in 1860 but rebuilt immediately thereafter. Nothing remains of this station today.

Ahnert (1973) and Talbot both identify the Gila Ranch Station as having been within Township 5S, Range 4W, Section 8. Using the centroid point of this quadrant as a reference, Gila Ranch would have been located in the vicinity of coordinates N33° 0' 26", W112° 41' 29".

In correspondence dated October 22, 2010, Ahnert stated that coordinates N33° 0' 26.19", W112° 41' 29.61" are within 3100 feet of his most recent location measurement.

The Wray / OCTA mapping data places the Gila Ranch site at coordinates N33° 0' 01.87", W112° 41' 55.83" -- in the far northwest corner of Township 5S, Range 4W, Section 8, the same section as was reported by Ahnert (1973 and 2011) and Talbot (1992). There appears to be unanimous agreement that the actual site of the Gila Ranch Station was at coordinates N33° 0' 01.87", W112° 41' 55.83"

Will C. Barnes in his 1983 book *Arizona's Names* notes of the town of Gila Bend:

> At the original location of Gila Bend, the freighting and mail station was called Gila Ranch. The name for the ranch on the site of the Maricopa Indian Village was noted in 1854 by Lt. Parke as being Tezotal, for the desert ironwood tree listed as *Olneya tesota* in Dr. John Torrey's botanical report for the Boundary Commission.
>
> At one time along the stream course was a South Gila Bend and North Gila Bend, about twenty miles apart. Both were probably in existence to serve emigrants. Papago Indians called the vicinity 'Petato,' their word for the familiar vegetable green called 'Lamb's Quarter,' which grew abundantly in the region.
>
> In 1865 ... a small community developed around the stage station named Gila Bend. In 1880 railroad tracks were completed and a station was built away from the river, although the steam engines drew water from the river until the railroad sank its own wells. When that

happened, the small community began relocating near the railroad. The first settler at the new town site (laid out by Daniel Murphy, John H. Martin, and William H. Barnes) was Daniel Noonan. Noonan had been postmaster at the Gila Bend post office at the river freighting and stage station. By 1910 all that remained of the older location were eight ... families.

Ormsby and Bailey both specifically cite the Gila Ranch station.

Another important resource to be considered in "tightening down" the Butterfield sites in this area is the Gila Bend Museum on South Pima Street in the modern community of Gila Bend -- approximate coordinates N32° 56' 50.16", W112° 43' 1.95".

References:

Ahnert, Gerald T.; *Retracing the Butterfield Overland Trail through Arizona; a Guide to the Route of 1857-1861;* Westernlore Press; Tucson AZ; 1973.

Bailey, Goddard; *California -- Arrival of the Overland Mail -- Itinerary of the Route*; as reported by newspaper article; *New York Times* (NY) - October 14, 1858.

Bailey, Goddard; *Report to Postmaster General A.V. Brown - Full itinerary as reported by De Bow's Review and Industrial Resources, Statistics etc.;* published by *De Bow's Review*; New Orleans and Washington City; 1858. See specifically *Internal Improvements - 1. Wagon Road to the Pacific*; pp. 719-721. Internet accessible at http://books.google.com/books?id=5CYoAAAAYAAJ&pg=PA720&lpg=PA720&dq=Cienega+de+los+Pimas&source=bl&ots=_5lZw_Bq23&sig=T6scCb8cpbY7KwjxpYoNvZpcgvI&hl=en&ei=i6KnS6KNOIr2M5yprIED&sa=X&oi=book_result&ct=result&resnum=2&ved=0CAwQ6AEwAQ#v=onepage&q=Cienega%20de%20los%20Pimas&f=false (accessed March 22, 2010).

Barnes, Will C.; *Arizona Place Names*; University of Arizona Press; Tucson AZ; 1960.

Conkling, Roscoe P. and Margaret B.; *The Butterfield Overland Mail, 1857–1869* (3 vols.); Glendale, CA: A. H. Clark Company, 1947.

Earthpoint; *Township and Range, Public Land Survey System on Google Earth*; internet data conversion system accessible at http://www.earthpoint.us/townships.aspx (accessed April 22, 2010).

National Park Service; *Juan Bautista de Anza National Historic Trail Guide (Maricopa County)*; Internet publication available at http://www.solideas.com/DeAnza/TrailGuide/ (accessed July 28, 2010).

Oregon - California Trails Association; *Learn. Connect. Preserve.*; Internet publication accessible at http://www.octa-trails.org/ (accessed October 9, 2010).

Ormsby, Waterman L.; *The Butterfield Overland Mail (Only Through Passenger on the First Westbound Stage)*; original publications *New York Herald* (NY) Sep 26 - Nov 19, 1858; republished by Henry E. Huntington Library and Art Gallery, San Marino CA, 1942 – 1998.

Talbot, Dan; *Historical Guide to the Mormon Battalion and Butterfield Trail;* Westernlore Press, 1992.

Gila Ranch to Oatman Flat

April 22, 2011

Gila Ranch (approximate per Talbot) - Gila Bend, AZ • Maricopa County
(N33° 0' 26.19", W112° 41' 29.61")

TO Oatman Grave / Oatman Flat - • Maricopa County AZ (N33° 0'
16.53", W113° 9' 10.85")

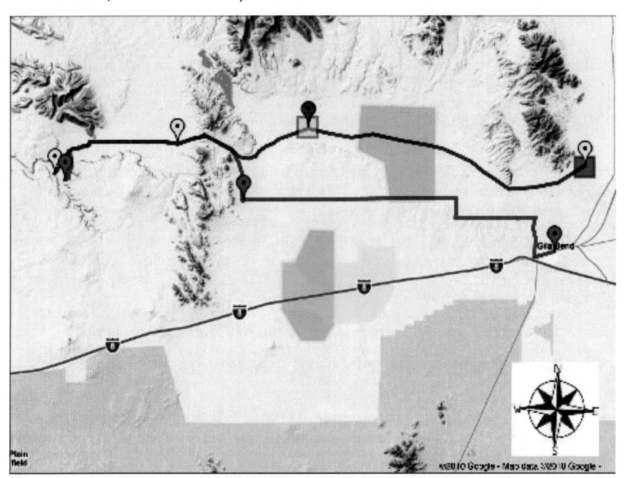

Approximate Actual Route, Gila Ranch to Oatman Flat

29.4 miles (1858 Bailey itinerary = 37 miles)

Secondary Landmarks:

Murderer's Grave per Ahnert (1973) - approximate coordinates N33° 2' 7.85",
W112° 56' 5.60"

Painted Rocks Historic Park - approximate coordinates N33° 1' 24.00", W113°
2' 55.00"

Notes:

The Butterfield Route through the segment from Gila Ranch to Oatman
Flat is somewhat easier to track than are the locations of the stations
themselves.

The ongoing Butterfield Route continues along the historical corridor
followed by Spanish explorer Juan Bautista de Anza (1775-1776); the
Mormon Battalion (1846-1847); the road established by Col. James B. Leach
(1857); and the course of the San Antonio - San Diego Stage route
established by Skillman, Wasson, Birch et al. (1857).

In modern context, Ahnert (1973 ad 2011) and Talbot (1992) include
detailed maps of the Gila Ranch to Oatman Flat Butterfield Route. Given
close comparison to one another, those maps clearly indicate an essentially
westward route as indicated in this report.

Talbot clearly shows this segment of the Butterfield Route as directly
tracking the earlier Mormon Battalion Route. He also indicates this route as
having been explored and mapped by John Russell Bartlett during his U.S. -
Mexico Boundary Survey as of June, 1852.

The Oregon - California Trails Association (OCTA) has also done a
significant amount of field research and mapping of this segment. That data;
supplied by Chris Wray of OCTA as of October 28, 2010; has also been taken
into account.

The detailed Wray / OCTA mapping data clearly indicates the essentially
westward route as outlined in this segment map and concurs with the route
reflected by Ahnert and Talbot.

Ormsby specifically mentions a station at "Murderer's Grave." On the
journey beyond Gila Ranch, he notes "The stations in the Gila Valley are from
fifteen to twenty miles apart. The first we touched at was called 'Murderer's
Grave.' It was the scene of the summary killing of a young man by a band of
emigrants, he having in a fit of passion shot a guardian who had him in
charge. His punishment was as summary as his crime, and his wealth did

not avail him to escape, as perhaps it might in a more 'civilized and enlightened community.'"

Bailey specifically cites Murderer's Grave as a mileage point and places it 17 miles from Gila Ranch.

According to Talbot's rendition of the Ormsby story, the name "Murderer's Grave" was derived from an incident in 1856: "It seems a young man traveling with his guardian camped on this spot and in a fit of passion shot and killed his guardian. Members of an emigrant train that arrived on the scene witnessed the crime and punished the young assassin by executing him on the spot. The young man, who was of a wealthy family from the East, was buried on the site alongside his victim."

Talbot and Ahnert say the stage station at Murderer's Grave was renamed Kenyon's Station after the Butterfield divisional supervisor for the area, one Marcus L. Kenyon. Nothing remains to locate the exact location of Murderer's Grave / Kenyon's Station.

Talbot places the Murderer's Grave / Kenyon site within the boundaries of Township 4S, Range 7W -- but does not offer a closer identification. Ahnert, however, specifies the site as being within Township 4S, Range 7W, Section 36. Plotted compared to the de Anza and Mormon Battalion routes and estimating this site at the center of quadrant described by Ahnert would place the Murderer's Grave site near coordinates N33° 2' 7.85", W112° 56' 5.60".

In correspondence dated October 22, 2010, Ahnert states that the coordinates at N33° 2' 7.85", W112° 56' 5.60" are within 3700 feet of his most recent site measurements.

The Wray / OCTA mapping data places Kenyon Station / Murderer's Grave at coordinates N33° 2' 08.89", W112° 55' 37.59", slightly east of the report coordinates within Township 4S, Range 7W, Section 36 as reported by Ahnert (1973).

• Data update as of March 2013 • Ahnert's 2011 publication concurs with the Wray / OCTA coordinates as does Fred Yeck's additional research. Thus, by default, it may be assumed that there coordinates are likely to be more accurate than the initial as determined in the preparation of this report. That said, however. The Ahnert / Wray /OCTA / Yeck coordinates are inaccessible by road. Thus, the report coordinates are about as close as you can get without taking a healthy desert hike.

There is an important intermediate location to the west of the Murderer's Grave location. Said site being the Painted Rocks Historic Park (approximate coordinates N33° 1' 24.00", W113° 2' 55.00").

While not a specifically Butterfield-related site, Painted Rocks is a clear indicator of the cultural importance of this route segment.

Painted Rocks is the site of numerous Indian pictographs, indicating an importance far predating the Butterfield and de Anza. It is operated as an historic site under the jurisdiction of the Bureau of Land Management and was added to the National Register of Historic Places (added 1977 - Site - #77000238).

According to information from the BLM, "Painted Rock Petroglyph Site, approximately 90 miles southwest of Phoenix, Arizona, provides visitors the opportunity to view an ancient archaeological site containing hundreds of symbolic and artistic rock etchings, or 'petroglyphs,' produced centuries ago by prehistoric peoples. There are also inscriptions made by people who passed through during historic times. Many well- known events in Arizona history occurred near the Petroglyph Site, including the expedition of Juan Bautista de Anza that founded San Francisco, the Mormon Battalion and the Butterfield Overland Mail. Formerly a unit of the Arizona State Park system, jurisdiction of Painted Rock Petroglyph Site reverted to the Bureau of Land Management in 1989."

The Oatman Flat Station is infamous for having been near the site of another tragic landmark – the location of a February 1851 massacre and abduction involving a Mormon emigrant family and renegade Indian tribesmen.

These are the details of the Oatman tragedy according to a synopsis from the city of Gila Bend:

> On August 10, 1850 Royce Oatman with his wife and seven children left Independence, Missouri, in a wagon train led by James C. Brewster, a member of the Church of Jesus Christ of Latter-Day Saints, whose disagreements with the church leadership in Salt Lake City, Utah, had caused him to break with Brigham Young and lead his followers to California. There were about fifty people in the nine-wagon party. The emigrants crossed into New Mexico where dissension caused the group to split near Santa Fe. Brewster headed North and Royce and several other families took the Southern route through Socorro, Santa Cruz and Tucson. Part of the company resolved to stay

in Tucson, and the rest proceeded down the Santa Cruz to the Gila and Pima Villages.

Against the advice of others, the Oatman family left the Pima Villages to make the trip down the Gila into California. At the site west of Gila Bend their wagon was too heavy to be pulled up the steep slope to the top of the mesa, so they unloaded it and moved the contents up by hand. While the Oatmans were resting on top, a group of Indians approached and asked for food. What they gave was not enough to satisfy the Indians, who then attacked. All of the family was killed with the exception of two daughters, Olive and Mary Ann, and a son, Lorenzo who was clubbed, thrown off the mesa, and left for dead.

Lorenzo survived and made it back to the Pima Villages and from there to California where he spent the next five years in an effort to find Olive and Mary Ann. Olive and Mary Ann were taken into captivity and sometime later the girls were traded to the Mohave Indian Tribe. Mary Ann died in captivity, but Olive survived and was ransomed in {February] 1856 by the United States Government at Ft. Yuma. [Soon] After Olive and Lorenzo were reunited they met Reverend R. B. Stratton, who prepared a book recounting their tale; this is the main source book on the massacre.

The City of Gila Bend information continues:

Both Olive and Lorenzo asserted that their attackers were Apache. However, in 1903, ethnographer A. C. Kroeber interviewed an Indian named Tokwaea, who claimed to have been one of the Mohave warriors who escorted Olive to Fort Yuma after her release. Tokwaea said the Indians who attacked the Oatmans were Yavapai.

The Bartlett Boundary Survey party came across the massacre site in the summer of 1852 and noted fragments of trunks, boxes, clothing, and human bones. In the fall of 1858, Waterman Ormsby, traveling on the first westbound Butterfield stage, reported seeing the graves of Royce Oatman and his wife.

Ormsby recounts the story of the Oatman Massacre and notes passing by the family gravesite near the Oatman Flat Station which he placed "about 22 miles distant" from Murderer's Grave. Bailey places the Oatman Flat Station as having been 20 miles west of Murderer's Grave.

Talbot reports that "Oatman Station ... was located in the flat close by the river. The exact spot is unknown and the main portion of the flat is under cultivation... The original emigrant road forded the [Gila] river above Oatman Flat and ran for about seven miles along the north side of the river, then recrossed to the south bank at the flat. In 1858 there was a stage station at Oatman Flat with a Mr. Jacobs as attendant."

For purposes of this report, we have used the Oatman Grave location (N33° 0' 16.53", W113° 9' 10.85"). In correspondence as of October 22, 2010, Ahnert reports that these coordinates are within 2000 feet of his most recent location measurements for the Oatman Flat Station.

The Wray / OCTA mapping data places the Oatman Flat Station slightly east of the Oatman gravesite according to GLO mapping data from the 1870s (coordinates N33° 0' 14.40", W113° 9' 21.60"). •Data update as of March 2013 • In his 2011 publication, Ahnert's specific coordinates for the Oatman Flat Station essentially concur with the Wray / OCTA coordinates.

References:

Ahnert, Gerald T.; *Retracing the Butterfield Overland Trail through Arizona; a Guide to the Route of 1857-1861;* Westernlore Press; Tucson AZ; 1973 and *The Butterfield Trail and Overland Mail Company in Arizona; 1858-1861*; Canastota Publishing Co, Canastota NY: 2011.

Bailey, Goddard; *California -- Arrival of the Overland Mail -- Itinerary of the Route*; as reported by newspaper article; *New York Times* (NY) - October 14, 1858.

Bailey, Goddard; *Report to Postmaster General A.V. Brown - Full itinerary as reported by De Bow's Review and Industrial Resources, Statistics etc.;* published by *De Bow's Review*; New Orleans and Washington City; 1858. See specifically *Internal Improvements - 1. Wagon Road to the Pacific*; pp. 719-721. Internet accessible at http://books.google.com/books?id=5CYoAAAAYAAJ&pg=PA720&lpg=PA720&dq=Cienega+de+los+Pimas&source=bl&ots=_5lZw_Bq23&sig=T6scCb8cpbY7KwjxpYoNvZpcgvI&hl=en&ei=i6KnS6KNOIr2M5yprIED&sa=X&oi=book_result&ct=result&resnum=2&ved=0CAwQ6AEwAQ#v=onepage&q=Cienega%20de%20los%20Pimas&f=false (accessed March 22, 2010).

Barnes, Will C.; *Arizona Place Names*; University of Arizona Press; Tucson AZ; 1960.

Conkling, Roscoe P. and Margaret B.; *The Butterfield Overland Mail, 1857–1869* (3 vols.); Glendale, CA: A. H. Clark Company, 1947.

Earthpoint; *Township and Range, Public Land Survey System on Google Earth*; internet data conversion system accessible at http://www.earthpoint.us/townships.aspx (accessed April 22, 2010).

National Park Service; *Juan Bautista de Anza National Historic Trail Guide Maricopa County AZ)*; Internet publication available at http://www.solideas.com/DeAnza/TrailGuide/Maricopa/index.htm\ (accessed July 28, 2010).

National Register of Historic Places; *National Register Locations by State*; Internet publication; accessible at

http://www.nationalregisterofhistoricplaces.com/state.html (accessed May 3, 2010).

Oregon - California Trails Association; *Learn. Connect. Preserve.*; Internet publication accessible at http://www.octa-trails.org/ (accessed October 9, 2010).

Ormsby, Waterman L.; *The Butterfield Overland Mail (Only Through Passenger on the First Westbound Stage)*; original publications *New York Herald* (NY) Sep 26 - Nov 19, 1858; republished by Henry E. Huntington Library and Art Gallery, San Marino CA, 1942 – 1998.

Talbot, Dan; *Historical Guide to the Mormon Battalion and Butterfield Trail;* Westernlore Press, 1992.

U.S. Department of the Interior - Bureau of Land Management; *Painted Rock Petroglyph Site*; Internet publication accessible at http://www.blm.gov/az/st/en/prog/recreation/camping/dev_camps/painted_rock.html (accessed July 28, 2010).

Oatman Flat to Flapjack Ranch

April 22, 2011

Oatman Grave / Oatman Flat - • Maricopa County AZ (N33° 0' 16.53", W113° 9' 10.85")

TO Flapjack Ranch / Stanwix Station - northeast of Dateland AZ • Yuma County (N32° 53' 28.34", W113° 26' 48.76")

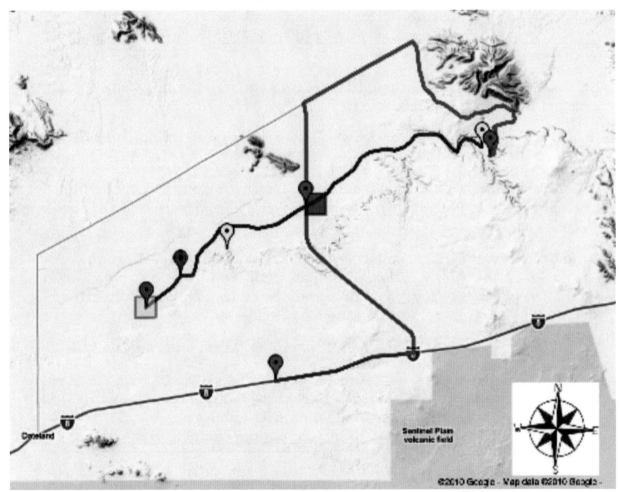

Approximate Actual Route, Oatman Flat to Flapjack Ranch

20.5 miles (1858 Bailey itinerary = 20 miles)

Secondary Landmarks:

Burke's Station (Agua Caliente) per Talbot - approximate coordinates N32° 57' 44.40", W113° 18' 21.24"

Sears Point - approximate coordinates N32° 55' 57.17", W113° 22' 30.68"

Stanwix (modern community) - approximate coordinates N32° 50' 20.07", W113° 19' 59.12"

Notes:

The ongoing Butterfield Route from Oatman Flat to Flapjack Ranch continues along the historical corridor followed by Spanish explorer Juan Bautista de Anza (1775-1776); the Mormon Battalion (1846-1847); the road established by Col. James B. Leach (1857); and the course of the San Antonio - San Diego Stageline established by Skillman, Wasson, Birch et al. (1857).

In modern context, Ahnert (1973 and 2011) and Talbot (1992) include detailed maps of the Oatman to Flapjack Butterfield Route. Compared closely to one another, those maps clearly indicate an essentially westward route along the Gila River.

Talbot clearly shows this segment of the Butterfield Route as directly tracking the earlier Mormon Battalion Route. He also indicates this route as having been explored and mapped by John Russell Bartlett during his U.S. - Mexico Boundary Survey as of June, 1852.

The Oregon - California Trails Association (OCTA) has also done a significant amount of field research and mapping of this segment. That data; supplied by Chris Wray of OCTA as of October 28, 2010; has also been taken into account. The detailed Wray / OCTA mapping data clearly indicates the essentially westward route along the Gila River as outlined in this segment map and concurs with the route reflected by Ahnert and Talbot.

While neither Ormsby nor Bailey mention it, later documentation indicates an intermediate station at Burke's Station (also known as Agua Caliente - approximate coordinates N32 57' 44.40", W113 18' 21.24")

Talbot notes that Burke's station was established in September, 1858, and named for station-keeper Patrick Burke. It was later purchased by William Fourr, who had also acquired the Oatman Flat station in 1864. He also reports that the Burke's station operated as a stage stop through 1874.

Ahnert (1973) and Talbot both place Burke's Station within the bounds of Township 5S, Range 10W, Section 28. Granger and Barnes, in their respective *Arizona Place Names* books, indicate that "Burke's Station" was an earlier name referring to Agua Caliente.

In correspondence dated October 22, 2010, Ahnert states that coordinates N32° 57' 44.40", W113° 18' 21.24" are within 3100 feet of his most recent coordinate measurements for the Burke's Station site.

The Wray / OCTA mapping data places the site at coordinates N32° 57' 52.50", W113° 17' 44.40" -- approximately 3200 feet northeast of the report coordinates and in concurrence with the description supplied by Ahnert (2010). • Data update as of March 2013 • In his 2011 publication, Ahnert concurs with the Wray /OCTA coordinates for Burke's Station. Fred Yeck's data and measurements concur as well.

The next landmark that helps us place the Butterfield Route is Sears Point (approximate coordinates N32° 55' 57.17", W113° 22' 30.68"). Sears Point is a prominent geological formation with long-standing spiritual and cultural importance to the native people of the area dating into prehistory. It was notable even in 1858 for the many Indian petroglyphs carved on the rocks in the area.

Talbot's maps clearly indicate Sears Point, although he shows the Butterfield Route passing to the south of the point. The Wray / OCTA mapping data places Sears Point at coordinates N32° 55' 57.58", W113° 22' 30.51" (approximately 0.3 mile south of the report coordinates. The Wray / OCTA mapping appears to indicate the route as passing immediately along the northern tip of Sears Point. Ahnert's maps (1973) do not specify Sears Point.

Today, the Sears Point area is an address restricted site of some 17,470 acres listed on the National Register of Historic Places (Sears Point Archaeological District - (added 1985 - #85003150). Because of the cultural importance of the petroglyphs, Sears Point is an Area of Critical Environmental Concern under the administration of the Bureau of Land Management.

There is a great deal of confusion regarding the name of the next Butterfield stop. Bailey refers to it as "Flapjack Ranch" in his mileage listings. Ormsby called it "The Dutchman's". The name "Stanwix Station" has also been used in contemporary local reports.

Talbot says the station was locally known as "Stanwix Station," but chronicles the other references to "Flapjack Ranch" and "Dutchman's". He reports that the station was the residence of Butterfield employee Wash Jacobs in 1860 and was then acquired by a substantial rancher in the area named King Woolsey in the late 1860s. Stanwix was the site of a Union / Confederate skirmish on March 15, 1862 and later became the location for a telegraph station.

Talbot does not list a township and range notation for this station. Ahnert (1973), however, lists the location as being within the bounds of Township 6S, Range 12W, Section 24 according to measurements initially reported by the Conklings.

Estimating the station location at the center of that quadrant would place it at coordinates N32° 53' 28.34", W113° 26' 48.76".

In correspondence dated October 22 - 25, 2010, Ahnert noted that more current research conducted in collaboration with Darryl Montgomery of the Arizona Historical Society indicates that the station site plotted by the Conklings and subsequently followed by Talbot and other researchers may have been erroneous. Ahnert noted that the actual Stanwix / Flapjack Ranch appears to have been about 2.4 miles northeast of coordinates N32° 53' 28.34", W113° 26' 48.76", which would place it in the vicinity of N32° 54' 49.32", W113° 24' 59.40".

Plotted as compared to GLO maps of the area as of the 1870s, the Wray / OCTA mapping data places Stanwix Station at coordinates N32° 54' 49.22", W113° 25' 02.18", which essentially concurs with Ahnert's placement as of 2010 -- approximately 2.4 miles northeast of the Ahnert (1973) location.

Additional research may be required for this station.

References:

Ahnert, Gerald T.; *Retracing the Butterfield Overland Trail through Arizona; a Guide to the Route of 1857-1861;* Westernlore Press; Tucson AZ; 1973 and *The Butterfield Trail and Overland Mail Company in Arizona; 1858-1861*; Canastota Publishing Co, Canastota NY: 2011.

Bailey, Goddard; *California -- Arrival of the Overland Mail -- Itinerary of the Route*; as reported by newspaper article; *New York Times* (NY) - October 14, 1858.

Bailey, Goddard; *Report to Postmaster General A.V. Brown - Full itinerary as reported by De Bow's Review and Industrial Resources, Statistics etc.;* published by *De Bow's Review*; New Orleans and Washington City; 1858. See specifically *Internal Improvements - 1. Wagon Road to the Pacific*; pp. 719-721. Internet accessible at http://books.google.com/books?id=5CYoAAAAYAAJ&pg=PA720&lpg=PA720& dq=Cienega+de+los+Pimas&source=bl&ots=_5lZw_Bq23&sig=T6scCb8cpbY7K wjxpYoNvZpcgvI&hl=en&ei=i6KnS6KNOIr2M5yprIED&sa=X&oi=book_result& ct=result&resnum=2&ved=0CAwQ6AEwAQ#v=onepage&q=Cienega%20de%20 los%20Pimas&f=false (accessed March 22, 2010).

Barnes, Will C.; *Arizona Place Names*; University of Arizona Press; Tucson AZ; 1960.

Conkling, Roscoe P. and Margaret B.; *The Butterfield Overland Mail, 1857–1869* (3 vols.); Glendale, CA: A. H. Clark Company, 1947.

Earthpoint; *Township and Range, Public Land Survey System on Google Earth*; internet data conversion system accessible at http://www.earthpoint.us/townships.aspx (accessed April 22, 2010).

Granger, Byrd Howell; *Arizona's Names - X Marks the Place, Historical Names of Places in Arizona;* Falconer Publishing Company, 1983.

National Park Service; *Juan Bautista de Anza National Historic Trail Guide Yuma County AZ*; Internet publication available at http://www.solideas.com/DeAnza/TrailGuide/Yuma/index.html (accessed July 28, 2010).

National Register of Historic Places; *National Register Locations by State*; Internet publication; accessible at

http://www.nationalregisterofhistoricplaces.com/state.html (accessed May 3, 2010).

Oregon - California Trails Association; *Learn. Connect. Preserve.*; Internet publication accessible at http://www.octa-trails.org/ (accessed October 9, 2010).

Ormsby, Waterman L.; *The Butterfield Overland Mail (Only Through Passenger on the First Westbound Stage)*; original publications *New York Herald* (NY) Sep 26 - Nov 19, 1858; republished by Henry E. Huntington Library and Art Gallery, San Marino CA, 1942 – 1998.

Talbot, Dan; *Historical Guide to the Mormon Battalion and Butterfield Trail;* Westernlore Press, 1992.

U.S. Department of the Interior - Bureau of Land Management; *Sears Point Archaeology - Historic Trails*; Internet publication accessible at http://www.blm.gov/az/st/en/prog/recreation/cultural/sears/hist_trails.html (accessed July 28, 2010).

**Vicinity of Flapjack Ranch / Stanwix Station
(N32.896, W113.442).
Photo by Fred Yeck (2011).**

Flapjack Ranch to Griswell's Station

April 22, 2011

Flapjack Ranch / Stanwix Station - northeast of Dateland AZ • Yuma County N32° 50' 20.07", W113° 19' 59.12"

TO Griswell's Station / Grinnell's Station / Texas Hill (approximate) – northwest of Dateland • Yuma County N32° 49' 50.01", W113° 39' 33.53"

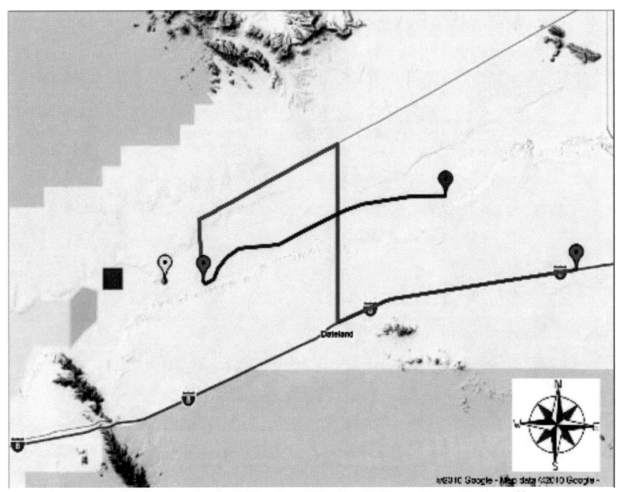

Approximate Actual Route, Flapjack Ranch to Griswell

13.75 miles (1858 Bailey itinerary = 15 miles)

Secondary Landmarks:

Texas Hill - geological landmark - approximate coordinates N32° 49' 53.17", W113° 41' 36.72"

Notes:

While the ongoing route of the Butterfield appears to be a fairly straightforward replication of the de Anza Trail, Mormon Battalion Route, etc. along the Gila River, the next station is known by many names. Bailey refers to the next station beyond Flapjack Ranch / Stanwix as "Griswell's". Bailey noted that Griswell's Station was 15 miles west of Flapjack Ranch.

Ormsby makes no mention of Griswell's Station. He does, however report that "A ride of 18 miles over a rough, stony and sandy road brought us to Texas Hill, near Pringle's Peak -- a rugged mount about 1,500 feet high -- which tapers down to the level of the plain, into which it juts like the nose of a swordfish. It is mainly composed of red slate rocks, and in the moonlight looks like a hill of icebergs."

Talbot does not mention "Griswell's" specifically. He places the next station at "Texas Hill" but offers few specifics as to the exact location.

Later researchers have variously referred to this station as "Griswell's", "Grinnell's", "Griswald's", and "Texas Hill" -- making it a bit difficult at times to properly incorporate research.

Given the multitude of names, however, we can still determine the route and the station location.

The Butterfield Route through this segment continues along the historical corridor followed by Spanish explorer Juan Bautista de Anza (1775-1776); the Mormon Battalion (1846-1847); the road established by Col. James B. Leach (1857); and the course of the San Antonio - San Diego Stage route established by Skillman, Wasson, Birch et al. (1857).

In modern context, Talbot (1992) includes detailed maps of the route and refers to the next station as "Texas Hill Camp". He clearly identifies this segment of the Butterfield Route as following the earlier Mormon Battalion Route through the area. Talbot also indicates this route as having been explored by John Russell Bartlett during his U.S. - Mexico Boundary Survey as of June, 1852.

Ahnert (1973 and 2011) includes detailed maps of this segment of the Butterfield Route as well. He refers to the next station as "Grinnell's", however.

The Ahnert (1973) and Talbot (1992) maps appear to identify the same station site under different names, and both clearly indicate a continuing west to southwest route along the Gila River.

The Oregon - California Trails Association (OCTA) has also done a significant amount of field research and mapping of this segment. That data, supplied by Chris Wray of OCTA as of October 28, 2010, has also been taken into account. The detailed Wray / OCTA mapping data clearly indicates the west to southwest route along the Gila River as outlined in this segment map and concurs with the route reflected by Ahnert and Talbot. That data identifies the station site as "Grinnell's".

As to the station site proper, Talbot mentions that the Texas Hill Station was "about two miles due east of a black pointed butte called Texas Hill" but does not cite township and range. That location compared to both Ormsby and Bailey would place the "Texas Hill Station" in the vicinity of coordinates N32° 49' 50", W113° 39' 33". Talbot also notes specifically that the Texas Hill area served as a campground for the Mormon Battalion (1846-1847).

Following the Conklings' lead, Ahnert (1973) specifically referred to "Grinnell's Station ... later known as Texas Hill Station" and placed the location within Township 7S, Range 14W, Section 7.

In correspondence dated October 22-25, 2010, Ahnert notes that ensuing field research into this location indicates that the Township 7S, Range 14W, Section 7 location (to the west of Texas Hill proper and based upon Conklings' data) was in error and may have been a later stage station rather than a Butterfield station. He stated that the correct Butterfield Station location was indeed to the east of Texas Hill.

For the purpose of this report, we have followed the "two miles east of Texas Hill" references to establish the approximated location of this station at coordinates N32° 49' 50", W113° 39' 33". During the 2010 correspondence, Ahnert confirmed the proper site as being within 2200 feet of these coordinates according to his most recent research and onsite measurements.

The Wray / OCTA mapping data places Grinnell's / Texas Hill at coordinates N32° 49' 33.02", W113° 39' 51.54" -- which appears to be consistent with the report coordinates and Ahnert's 2010 description.

• Data update as of March 2013 • Ahnert's 2011 publication cites the proper location of Griswell / Grinnell / Texas Hill Station I concurrence with the Wray / OCTA coordinates. Yeck's coordinates concur to within a precious few feet.

References:

Ahnert, Gerald T.; *Retracing the Butterfield Overland Trail through Arizona; a Guide to the Route of 1857-1861;* Westernlore Press; Tucson AZ; 1973 and *The Butterfield Trail and Overland Mail Company in Arizona; 1858-1861*; Canastota Publishing Co, Canastota NY: 2011.

Bailey, Goddard; *California -- Arrival of the Overland Mail -- Itinerary of the Route*; as reported by newspaper article; *New York Times* (NY) - October 14, 1858.

Bailey, Goddard; *Report to Postmaster General A.V. Brown - Full itinerary as reported by De Bow's Review and Industrial Resources, Statistics etc.;* published by *De Bow's Review*; New Orleans and Washington City; 1858. See specifically *Internal Improvements - 1. Wagon Road to the Pacific*; pp. 719-721. Internet accessible at http://books.google.com/books?id=5CYoAAAAYAAJ&pg=PA720&lpg=PA720& dq=Cienega+de+los+Pimas&source=bl&ots=_5lZw_Bq23&sig=T6scCb8cpbY7K wjxpYoNvZpcgvI&hl=en&ei=i6KnS6KNOIr2M5yprIED&sa=X&oi=book_result& ct=result&resnum=2&ved=0CAwQ6AEwAQ#v=onepage&q=Cienega%20de%20 los%20Pimas&f=false (accessed March 22, 2010).

Conkling, Roscoe P. and Margaret B.; *The Butterfield Overland Mail, 1857–1869* (3 vols.); Glendale, CA: A. H. Clark Company, 1947.

National Park Service; *Juan Bautista de Anza National Historic Trail Guide Yuma County AZ)*; Internet publication available at http://www.solideas.com/DeAnza/TrailGuide/Yuma/index.html (accessed July 28, 2010).

Oregon - California Trails Association; *Learn. Connect. Preserve.*; Internet publication accessible at http://www.octa-trails.org/ (accessed October 9, 2010).

Ormsby, Waterman L.; *The Butterfield Overland Mail (Only Through Passenger on the First Westbound Stage)*; original publications *New York Herald* (NY) Sep 26 - Nov 19, 1858; republished by Henry E. Huntington Library and Art Gallery, San Marino CA, 1942 – 1998.

Talbot, Dan; *Historical Guide to the Mormon Battalion and Butterfield Trail;* Westernlore Press, 1992.

Griswell's Station to Peterman's Station

April 23, 2011

Texas Hill / Griswell's Station / Grinnell's Station (approximate) - northwest of Dateland AZ • Yuma County (N32° 49' 50.01", W113° 39' 33.53")

TO Peterman's Station - south of Norton AZ (N32° 47' 9.82", W113° 47' 55.39")

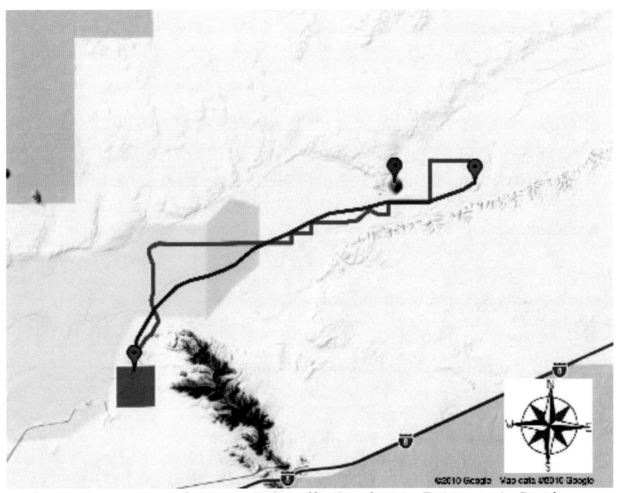

Approximate Actual Route, Griswell's Station to Peterman's Station 11.25 miles. (1858 Bailey itinerary = 12 miles)

Secondary Landmarks:

Texas Hill - geological landmark - approximate coordinates N32° 49' 53.17", W113° 41' 36.72"

Notes:

The continuing Butterfield Route from Griswell's Station/ Grinnell's / Texas Hill to Peterman's Station continues to track a southwesterly course along the south bank of the Gila River following the historical corridor used by Spanish explorer Juan Bautista de Anza (1775-1776); the Mormon Battalion (1846-1847); the road established by Col. James B. Leach (1857); and the course of the San Antonio - San Diego Stageline established by Skillman, Wasson, Birch et al. (1857).

In modern context, Ahnert (1973 and 2011) and Talbot (1992) include detailed maps of the Texas Hill to Peterman's Station Butterfield Route. Comparison of those maps to one another clearly indicates a slightly southwestward route along the Gila River.

Talbot clearly identifies this segment of the Butterfield Route as following the earlier Mormon Battalion Route through the area. Talbot also indicates this route as having been explored by John Russell Bartlett during his U.S. - Mexico Boundary Survey as of June, 1852.

The Oregon - California Trails Association (OCTA) has also done a significant amount of field research and mapping of this segment. That data; supplied by Chris Wray of OCTA as of October 28, 2010; has also been taken into account. The detailed Wray / OCTA mapping data clearly indicates the southwestward route along the south bank of the Gila River as outlined in this segment map and concurs with the route reflected by Ahnert and Talbot.

As to the Peterman's Station site -- Ormsby makes no mention of it, but Bailey cites it as a mileage point.

Talbot places Peterman's Station "on the west side of the north point of the Mohawk Mountains" in Township 8S, Range 15W, Section 4. Ahnert (1973) reports the same township, range and section data reported by Talbot. Locating a point within this quadrant toward "the west side of the north point of the Mohawk Mountains" places the station site in the vicinity of coordinates N32° 45' 54.56, W113° 48' 28.38".

In correspondence dated October 22 - 25, 2010, Ahnert states that coordinates N32° 45' 54.56", W113° 48' 28.38" are within 300 feet of the station site according to his most recent site measurements.

The Wray / OCTA mapping data places Peterman's Station at coordinates N32° 45' 44.90", W113° 48' 40.55" -- less than one mile southwest of the report coordinates as confirmed by Ahnert. • Data update as of March 2013 • Ahnert's publication as of 2011 again confirms this vicinity, as does data from Fred Yeck.

Talbot notes of Peterman's Station that "Little is known of the station's namesake ... He was located in the area as early as August 1857 and may have departed before the line was abandoned in spring 1861. In 1860 the station's name was changed to Mohawk, a name derived from the mountain range nearby."

Talbot also reports the Peterman structures as having been "two adobe buildings about twenty by twelve feet, connected by a passageway fifteen feet wide." He says the operators of the later Mohawk Station built another set of structures about ten feet from the original Peterman's, "each building being twenty-four by fifteen feet with a ten foot passageway. Each building contained two rooms and each room had a fireplace."

As of 1992, according to Talbot, only one adobe wall remained from the Mohawk structure at the station site.

References:

Ahnert, Gerald T.; *Retracing the Butterfield Overland Trail through Arizona; a Guide to the Route of 1857-1861;* Westernlore Press; Tucson AZ; 1973 and *The Butterfield Trail and Overland Mail Company in Arizona; 1858-1861*; Canastota Publishing Co, Canastota NY: 2011.

Bailey, Goddard; *California -- Arrival of the Overland Mail -- Itinerary of the Route*; as reported by newspaper article; *New York Times* (NY) - October 14, 1858.

Bailey, Goddard; *Report to Postmaster General A.V. Brown - Full itinerary as reported by De Bow's Review and Industrial Resources, Statistics etc.;* published by *De Bow's Review*; New Orleans and Washington City; 1858. See specifically *Internal Improvements - 1. Wagon Road to the Pacific*; pp. 719-721. Internet accessible at http://books.google.com/books?id=5CYoAAAAYAAJ&pg=PA720&lpg=PA720&dq=Cienega+de+los+Pimas&source=bl&ots=_5lZw_Bq23&sig=T6scCb8cpbY7KwjxpYoNvZpcgvI&hl=en&ei=i6KnS6KNOIr2M5yprIED&sa=X&oi=book_result&ct=result&resnum=2&ved=0CAwQ6AEwAQ#v=onepage&q=Cienega%20de%20los%20Pimas&f=false (accessed March 22, 2010).

Barnes, Will C.; *Arizona Place Names*; University of Arizona Press; Tucson AZ; 1960.

Conkling, Roscoe P. and Margaret B.; *The Butterfield Overland Mail, 1857–1869* (3 vols.); Glendale, CA: A. H. Clark Company, 1947.

Earthpoint; *Township and Range, Public Land Survey System on Google Earth*; internet data conversion system accessible at http://www.earthpoint.us/townships.aspx (accessed April 22, 2010).

National Park Service; *Juan Bautista de Anza National Historic Trail Guide, Yuma County AZ)*; Internet publication available at http://www.solideas.com/DeAnza/TrailGuide/Yuma/index.html (accessed July 28, 2010).

Oregon - California Trails Association; *Learn. Connect. Preserve.*; Internet publication accessible at http://www.octa-trails.org/ (accessed October 9, 2010).

Ormsby, Waterman L.; *The Butterfield Overland Mail (Only Through Passenger on the First Westbound Stage)*; original publications *New York Herald* (NY) Sep 26 - Nov 19, 1858; republished by Henry E. Huntington Library and Art Gallery, San Marino CA, 1942 – 1998.

Talbot, Dan; *Historical Guide to the Mormon Battalion and Butterfield Trail;* Westernlore Press, 1992.

Peterman's Station to Filibuster Camp

April 23, 2011

Peterman's Station - south of Norton • Yuma County (N32° 47' 9.82", W113° 47' 55.39")

TO Filibuster Camp - Wellton • Yuma County (N32° 41' 8.18", W114° 5' 57.61")

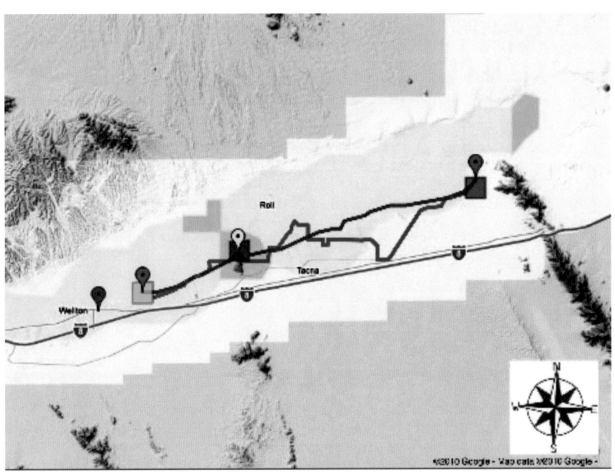

Approximate Actual Route, Peterman's Station to Filibuster

Camp 18.5 miles (1858 Bailey itinerary = 19 miles)

Secondary Landmarks:

Antelope Hill / Antelope Peak - near Wellton - approximate coordinates N32° 42' 47.17", W114° 0' 54.30"

Wellton Pioneer Museum - 10402 Fresno Street, Wellton - approximate coordinates N32° 40' 17.58", W114° 8' 17.92"

Notes:

The continuing Butterfield Route from Peterman's Station to Filibuster Camp continues to track a southwesterly course near the south bank of the Gila River along the historical corridor followed by Spanish explorer Juan Bautista de Anza (1775-1776); the Mormon Battalion (1846-1847); the road established by Col. James B. Leach (1857); and the course of the San Antonio - San Diego Stageline established by Skillman, Wasson, Birch et al. (1857).

In modern context, Ahnert (1973) and Talbot (1992) include detailed maps of the Peterman's Station to Filibuster Camp Butterfield Route. Comparison of those maps to one another clearly indicates the slightly southwestward route near the Gila River.

Talbot clearly identifies this segment of the Butterfield Route as following the earlier Mormon Battalion Route through the area. Talbot also indicates this route as having been explored by John Russell Bartlett during his U.S. - Mexico Boundary Survey as of June, 1852.

The Oregon - California Trails Association (OCTA) has also done a significant amount of field research and mapping of this segment. That data; supplied by Chris Wray of OCTA as of October 28, 2010; has also been taken into account. The detailed Wray / OCTA mapping data clearly indicates the same southwestward route as outlined in this segment map and concurs with the route reflected by Ahnert and Talbot.

There is an intermediate station site known as Antelope Hill along this segment of the route (established 1859 - approximate coordinates N32° 42' 47.17", W114° 0' 54.30").

Ahnert (1973 ad 2011) maintains that the Antelope Hill Station was "constructed in 1859 by the Butterfield Overland Company" and "took the place of Filibuster Camp because there was a better water supply at the site".

Ahnert places Antelope Hill Station within Township 8S, Range 17W, Section 21. Helping to place the exact coordinates for Antelope Hill, Talbot specifically reports that "As with other old stage stations, the railroad tracks supposedly pass directly over the station site." Following the Conklings' lead regarding Antelope Hill, he notes that "This station does not appear as one of the original Butterfield stations although it was a stopping place on Birch's [James E. Birch, San Antonio - San Diego Stage Line] route in 1857. In 1859, however, Antelope Peak did appear on the itinerary and Filibuster Camp ... was omitted."

That description within Ahnert's township / range / section description compared to the known de Anza and Mormon Battalion routes help to place an approximate site for this station near coordinates N32° 42' 47.17", W114° 0' 54.30". In correspondence dated October 22, 2010, Ahnert places these coordinates within 300 feet of his most recent site measurements.

The Wray / OCTA mapping data places Antelope Station at coordinates N32° 42' 46.34", W114° 0' 53.47" which clearly concurs with the report coordinates.

• Data update as of March 2013 • Ahnert's publication as of 2011 and data from Fred Yeck both essentially concur with Wray / OCTA that the site of the Antelope Hill Station was at coordinates N32° 42' 47.17", W114° 0' 54.30".

Ormsby does not mention the stations at Antelope Hill or Filibuster Camp. Bailey does not mention Antelope Hill, but cites Filibuster Camp as a mileage point.

Ahnert (1973) and Talbot (1992) both place the Filibuster Camp Station within Township 8S, Range 18W, Section 34. For the purpose of this report, we have used the centroid of this section for approximate station coordinates (N32° 41' 8.18", W114° 5' 57.61"). In correspondence dated October 22, 2010, Ahnert confirmed these coordinates as being within 70 feet of his most recent site measurements.

The Wray / OCTA mapping data places Filibuster Camp at coordinates N32° 41' 15.87", W114° 6' 12.56" -- slightly southeast of the report coordinates.

• Data update as of March 2013 • Ahnert's publication as of 2011 and data from Fred Yeck both essentially concur with that the site of the Filibuster Camp was at coordinates N32° 41' 8.18", W114° 5' 57.61"

Filibuster Camp was established in 1857 in conjunction with an ill-fated intrigue led by one Henry A. Crabb of California and backed by several prominent California politicos and leaders.

In March of that year, Crabb and the others formed an invasion party to enter Mexico -- purportedly to aid Mexican General Ignacio Pesqueira in Sonora state. Pesqueira was embroiled at the time in a power struggle with Governor Manuel María Gándara. Supposedly, the Californians were promised a strip of Mexican land along the Arizona border in exchange for aiding Pesqueira. Which section they then intended to secede from Mexico and annex into the United States. The "deal" (allegedly) was that Crabb et al. were to raise an army of 1,000 to aid Pesqueira in exchange for the land grant.

A smaller-than-expected expedition of Americans was enlisted and made camp at the site that would become "Filibuster Camp." Twenty men remained at the camp as a mere 68 made the march into Mexico -- only to find that Pesqueira was in control of the area, had already denounced the Californians' expedition as an invasion and laid ambush to halt the Californians' advance.

Making a long story short, Pesqueira's public denunciation urged the people of Sonora "to chastise with all the fury that can scarcely be contained in a heart swelling with resentment against coercion, the savage filibuster who has dared, in an unhappy hour, to tread our nation's soil and to arouse, insensate, our wrath. Let it die like a wild beast."

Crabb and all but one 15-year-old boy in his party were executed by Pesqueira. Crabb's head, preserved in a jar of tequila, was sent to Mexico City as a proof of Pesqueira's fealty to the government and his success in quelling the "invasion."

The town of Wellton, Arizona, is very definite about its proximity to Filibuster Camp and its status as a Butterfield location. Information from the town of Wellton states "We have a rich western history stemming from our roots as a water stop for the railroad (hence Well Town - Wellton) and the Butterfield Stage Coach." It continues:

Wellton, founded in 1878 and incorporated in 1970, lies 29 miles east of Yuma, Arizona. ...

Wellton (originally Well Town) was named for the time when water wells were drilled to service the Southern Pacific Railroad. Most areas were settled in the 1860's as the need arose for stations to serve the Butterfield Overland Mail stagecoaches. With the railroads eventually supplanting the stagecoach lines in the 1870's, several communities were established (Tacna and Wellton) to provide water facilities for the old steam-powered engines. As the stagecoach gave way to the railroad, so the railroad gave way to the automobile. Though rail service is still maintained through Wellton - Mohawk Valley, the current economic livelihood is based on agriculture.

The town also has an excellent small museum that includes among its holdings an original Butterfield coach and some adobe blocks from the original Filibuster Camp station. The Pioneer Museum is located at 10402 Fresno Street in Wellton.

References:

Ahnert, Gerald T.; *Retracing the Butterfield Overland Trail through Arizona; a Guide to the Route of 1857-1861;* Westernlore Press; Tucson AZ; 1973 and *The Butterfield Trail and Overland Mail Company in Arizona; 1858-1861*; Canastota Publishing Co, Canastota NY: 2011.

Bailey, Goddard; *California -- Arrival of the Overland Mail -- Itinerary of the Route*; as reported by newspaper article; *New York Times* (NY) - October 14, 1858.

Bailey, Goddard; *Report to Postmaster General A.V. Brown - Full itinerary as reported by De Bow's Review and Industrial Resources, Statistics etc.;* published by *De Bow's Review*; New Orleans and Washington City; 1858. See specifically *Internal Improvements - 1. Wagon Road to the Pacific*; pp. 719-721. Internet accessible at
http://books.google.com/books?id=5CYoAAAAYAAJ&pg=PA720&lpg=PA720&dq=Cienega+de+los+Pimas&source=bl&ots=_5lZw_Bq23&sig=T6scCb8cpbY7K wjxpYoNvZpcgvI&hl=en&ei=i6KnS6KNOIr2M5yprIED&sa=X&oi=book_result&

ct=result&resnum=2&ved=0CAwQ6AEwAQ#v=onepage&q=Cienega%20de%20los%20Pimas&f=false (accessed March 22, 2010).

Conkling, Roscoe P. and Margaret B.; *The Butterfield Overland Mail, 1857–1869* (3 vols.); Glendale, CA: A. H. Clark Company, 1947.

Earthpoint; *Township and Range, Public Land Survey System on Google Earth*; internet data conversion system accessible at http://www.earthpoint.us/townships.aspx (accessed April 22, 2010).

National Park Service; *Juan Bautista de Anza National Historic Trail Guide, Yuma County AZ)*; Internet publication available at http://www.solideas.com/DeAnza/TrailGuide/Yuma/index.html (accessed July 28, 2010).

Oregon - California Trails Association; *Learn. Connect. Preserve.*; Internet publication accessible at http://www.octa-trails.org/ (accessed October 9, 2010).

Ormsby, Waterman L.; *The Butterfield Overland Mail (Only Through Passenger on the First Westbound Stage)*; original publications *New York Herald* (NY) Sep 26 - Nov 19, 1858; republished by Henry E. Huntington Library and Art Gallery, San Marino CA, 1942 – 1998.

Talbot, Dan; *Historical Guide to the Mormon Battalion and Butterfield Trail;* Westernlore Press, 1992.

Wellton (AZ), Town of; About the Town of Wellton; Internet publication accessible at http://www.town.wellton.az.us/about.htm (accessed August 8, 2010).

Filibuster Camp to Swiveller's Ranch

April 23, 2011

Filibuster Camp - Wellton AZ • Yuma County (N32° 41' 8.18", W114° 5' 57.61")

TO Snively's (a.k.a. "Swiveller's") Ranch / Gila City – near Dome AZ • Yuma County (N32° 45' 18.47", W114° 21' 39.71")

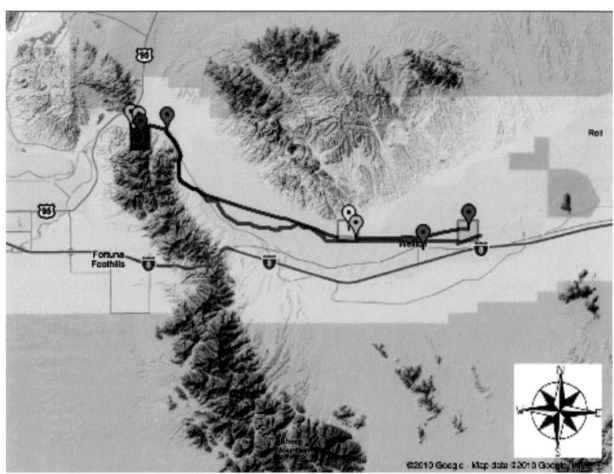

Approximate Actual Route, Filibuster Station to Snively's

Ranch 19.4 miles (1858 Bailey itinerary = 18 miles)

Secondary Landmarks:

Mission Camp per Ahnert (1973) and Talbot (1992) - near Wellton - approximate coordinates N32° 41' 7.24", W114° 12' 8.74"

Mission Camp per Wray - coordinates N32° 40' 42.96", W114° 11' 45.89"

Notes:

From Filibuster Camp to the west, the Butterfield Route tracks a westerly to northwesterly course near the Gila River along the historical corridor followed by Spanish explorer Juan Bautista de Anza (1775-1776); the Mormon Battalion (1846-1847); the road established by Col. James B. Leach (1857); and the course of the San Antonio - San Diego Stageline established by Skillman, Wasson, Birch et al. (1857).

In modern context, Ahnert (1973) and Talbot (1992) include detailed maps of the Butterfield Route from Filibuster Camp to the next major site at Snively's Ranch / Gila City. Comparison of these maps to one another clearly indicates this westerly to northwesterly route.

Talbot clearly identifies this segment of the Butterfield Route as following the earlier Mormon Battalion Route through the area. Talbot also indicates this route as having been explored by John Russell Bartlett during his U.S. - Mexico Boundary Survey as of June, 1852.

The Oregon - California Trails Association (OCTA) has also done a significant amount of field research and mapping of this segment. That data; supplied by Chris Wray of OCTA as of October 28, 2010; has also been taken into account. The detailed Wray / OCTA mapping data clearly indicates the same route as outlined in this segment map and concurs with the route reflected by Ahnert and Talbot.

There is an intermediate station site known as Mission Camp along this segment of the route (established 1859 - approximate coordinates N32° 41' 7.24", N114° 12' 8.74").

Regarding the Mission Camp Station, Talbot reports that this station was established upon the closure of Filibuster Camp. "It was thought to be built on the site of one of Father Kino's old missions, which were built between 1694 and 1706. Reports have been heard of finding old Spanish coins in the melted down adobes surrounding the immediate area. Mission Camp was established in the latter part of 1859 when Filibuster was abandoned. ... Nothing remains of the old station today."

Ahnert (1973 and 2011) and Talbot both place Mission Camp within the bounds of Township 8S, Range 19W, Section 34. For the purpose of this report, we have used the centroid point of that section for the approximate location of Mission Camp (coordinates N32° 41' 7.24", W114° 12' 8.74").

In correspondence dated October 22 - 25, 2010, Ahnert indicates the exact location of the Mission Camp site is located "about three miles away" from the report coordinates but did not offer a specific placement.

The Wray / OCTA mapping data places Mission Camp at coordinates N32° 40' 42.96", W114° 11' 45.89". • Data update as of March 2013 • Additional research may be required for the Mission Camp location. Yeck places the site slightly west at coordinates N32° 40' 40", W114° 13' 26". Ahnert 2011 places it further west at coordinates N32° 40' 26", W114° 14' 45".

As regards the next station, Bailey cites "Swiveller's Ranch" specifically as a mileage point. Ormsby does not specifically name "Swiveller's Ranch", but notes a station "twenty miles from Fort Yuma."

Regarding the route approaching Snively's Station, some modern commercial maps include a segment identified as "Route of Butterfield Stage" beginning at about South Avenue 17 E and East County 8th Street. That identified section follows the (later) Southern Pacific railroad tracks through into Yuma.

Talbot reports that the "Swiveller's Ranch" location was the home of Jacob Snively and was also referred to as "Snively's Ranch". Snively was a native Pennsylvanian, veteran of Texas' War of Independence and personal secretary to General Sam Houston. He is also reported to have been the first to find placer gold (gold recovered from riverbeds) in the Yuma area. His 1858 find reportedly started a mini-rush into the area.

The Texas State Historical Association's *Handbook of Texas* confirms Talbot's basic details regarding Jacob Snively's life and notes particularly:

> When gold was discovered in California in 1848, Snively, then living in Corpus Christi, turned his interests over to his brother David and crossed northern Mexico in 1849, to sail from Mazatlán to the gold fields of California. He searched for gold there until 1858, when he moved to Arizona Territory, where he discovered the "Placers of the Gila" on the Gila River some twenty-four miles east of Yuma. He was also involved in the discovery of the Castle Dome silver mines in Yuma County and took a leading role in organizing the district in conjunction with Hermann V. Ehrenberg.

After the first territorial election in Arizona, Governor John Noble Goodwin appointed Snively judge of Precinct Two of Council District Two. In the second half of the 1860s Snively prospected in New Mexico and Nevada, where he alternately found and lost small fortunes.

Snively was exploring a route from the site of present-day Phoenix, near which he was then living, when his group was attacked by an estimated 150 Apache Indians at the White Picacho, a noted landmark near Wickenburg, Arizona, on March 27, 1871. Snively was mortally wounded and abandoned by his companions. His body, badly decomposed and partially devoured by wild animals, was buried near the sandy arroyo where it fell. His remains were exhumed eight years later and reinterred near the mining settlement of Gillett, Arizona. Gillett has since become a ghost town, and Snively's grave is said to be unmarked. Snively Holes, a watering place east of Bill Williams Mountains, Arizona [near Lake Havasu City], is named for him."

Snively reportedly founded a town at the site of his ranch near Yuma in late 1858 and named it Gila City, but the quantity of recoverable gold in the area proved inadequate to maintain the settlement and the town was short-lived.

Local research indicates that a post office was established at Gila City in 1858. That post office closed in 1863 and was reopened in 1892 at the nearby railroad town of Dome. The Gila City / Dome post office had a spotty history -- opening and closing several times -- and was finally abandoned in 1940. There are nominal remnants of two adobe buildings at this location but it is uncertain whether they date from the Butterfield period or later.

Talbot quotes the 1864 writings of traveler J. Ross Browne (who had camped in the area for a time), "At one time over a thousand hardy adventurers were prospecting the gulches and canons in this vicinity. ... There was everything in Gila City within a few months but a church and a jail, which were accounted (as) barbarisms by the mass of the population. When the city was built, barrooms and billiard saloons opened, monte tables established, and all the accommodations necessary for civilized society placed upon a firm basis, the gold placers gave out. In other words, they had never give in [sic] anything of account. There was 'pay-dirt' back in the hills, but it didn't pay to carry it down to the river and wash it out by any ordinary process. Gila City collapsed. In the space of about a week it existed only in the memory of disappointed speculators. At the time of our visit, the promising Metropolis of Arizona consisted of three chimneys and a coyote."

Ahnert (1973) also refers to "Snively's Ranch." He does not cite township /range / section either. However, he definitively places the station in the vicinity (possibly slightly west) of Dome AZ.

In correspondence dated October 22 - 25, 2010, Ahnert notes that there is still confusion regarding the exact placement of Snively's / Swiveller's Ranch. He notes that Dome may have been a latter Butterfield stage station -- but that the original station was more likely located in the vicinity of the earlier Gila City mining camp location.

The original location of Snively's "Gila City" settlement is difficult to determine. Mining records for the area, however, indicate the majority of placer gold strikes (and establishment of the initial town / mining camp) to have been along Monitor Gulch within Township 8S, Range 21W, Section 11 (to the west of Dome AZ). The known route of the Butterfield Mail enters this quadrant near the northeast corner.

The Wray / OCTA mapping data specifically places "Snively's Station" at coordinates N32° 45' 19.72", W114° 23' 08.51" -- within Township 8S, Range 21W, Section 11. That data also specifically notes a location for Gila City given comparison to and overlay of 1870s GLO maps at coordinates N32° 45' 26.17", W114° 23' 33.24". The Gila City location is in the far northwest corner of Township 8S, Range 21W, Section 11.

• Data update as of March 2013 • I his 2011 publication, Ahnert suggests that the initial Swiveller / Snively Station was at Gila City in accord with the Wray / OCTA coordinates but that it was moved shortly thereafter to the eastern Dome AZ location. Yeck cites only the Dome AZ site. Here again, there seems to be consensus that the initial station was at the Gila City campo site ad was moved in 1858 to the Dome AZ location.

The coordinates used for Swiveller's Ranch / Snively's Ranch in this report represent the currently mappable location of Dome at coordinates N32° 45' 18.47", W114° 21' 39.71". The continuing route, however, passes through the probable earlier location of Gila City to the west.

References:

Ahnert, Gerald T.; *Retracing the Butterfield Overland Trail through Arizona; a Guide to the Route of 1857-1861;* Westernlore Press; Tucson AZ; 1973 and *The Butterfield Trail and Overland Mail Company in Arizona; 1858-1861*; Canastota Publishing Co, Canastota NY: 2011.

Bailey, Goddard; *California -- Arrival of the Overland Mail -- Itinerary of the Route*; as reported by newspaper article; *New York Times* (NY) - October 14, 1858.

Bailey, Goddard; *Report to Postmaster General A.V. Brown - Full itinerary as reported by De Bow's Review and Industrial Resources, Statistics etc.;* published by *De Bow's Review*; New Orleans and Washington City; 1858. See specifically *Internal Improvements - 1. Wagon Road to the Pacific*; pp. 719-721. Internet accessible at http://books.google.com/books?id=5CYoAAAAYAAJ&pg=PA720&lpg=PA720&dq=Cienega+de+los+Pimas&source=bl&ots=_5lZw_Bq23&sig=T6scCb8cpbY7K wjxpYoNvZpcgvI&hl=en&ei=i6KnS6KNOIr2M5yprIED&sa=X&oi=book_result& ct=result&resnum=2&ved=0CAwQ6AEwAQ#v=onepage&q=Cienega%20de%20 los%20Pimas&f=false (accessed March 22, 2010).

Conkling, Roscoe P. and Margaret B.; *The Butterfield Overland Mail, 1857–1869* (3 vols.); Glendale, CA: A. H. Clark Company, 1947.

Earthpoint; *Township and Range, Public Land Survey System on Google Earth*; internet data conversion system accessible at http://www.earthpoint.us/townships.aspx (accessed April 22, 2010).

National Park Service; *Juan Bautista de Anza National Historic Trail Guide Yuma County AZ)*; Internet publication available at http://www.solideas.com/DeAnza/TrailGuide/Yuma/index.html (accessed July 28, 2010).

Oregon - California Trails Association; *Learn. Connect. Preserve.*; Internet publication accessible at http://www.octa-trails.org/ (accessed October 9, 2010).

Ormsby, Waterman L.; *The Butterfield Overland Mail (Only Through Passenger on the First Westbound Stage)*; original publications *New York Herald* (NY) Sep 26 - Nov 19, 1858; republished by Henry E. Huntington Library and Art Gallery, San Marino CA, 1942 – 1998.

Talbot, Dan; *Historical Guide to the Mormon Battalion and Butterfield Trail;* Westernlore Press, 1992.

Texas State Historical Association; *Handbook of Texas - Snively, Jacob*; internet publication accessible at http://www.tshaonline.org/handbook/online/articles/fsn07 (accessed April 23, 2011).

Swiveller's Ranch (Arizona) to Fort Yuma (California)

April 23, 2011

Snively's (a.k.a. "Swiveller's") Ranch / Gila City – near Dome AZ • Yuma County (N32° 45' 18.47", W114° 21' 39.71")

TO Fort Yuma - Winterhaven CA • Imperial County (N32° 43' 54.17", W114° 36' 55.83")

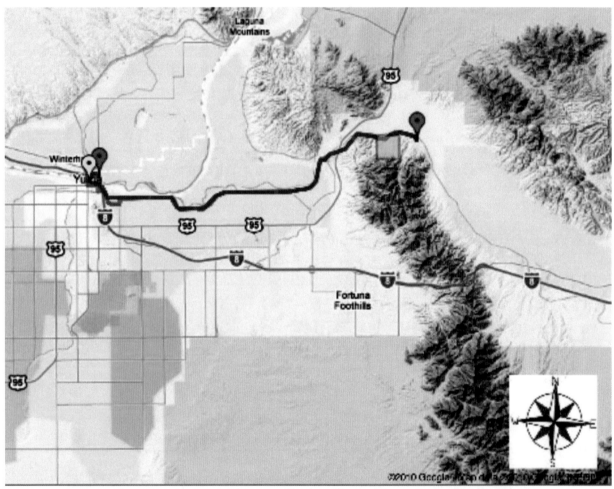

Approximate Actual Route, Swiveller's Ranch to Fort Yuma

18.5 miles (1858 Bailey itinerary = 20 miles)

Secondary Landmarks:

Gila City / Monitor Gulch mining camp area - Township 8S, Range 21W, Section 11 - northwest corner - coordinates N32° 45' 27.51", W114° 23' 33.28"

Yuma Crossing - Yuma Crossing State Historical Park / Yuma Quartermaster Depot State Historic Park - coordinates N32 43' 32.27", W114 37' 19.42"

Notes:

From Snively's / Swiveller's Ranch / Gila City onward to Fort Yuma, the Butterfield Route tracks a southwesterly to westerly course near the Gila River along the historical corridor followed by Spanish explorer Juan Bautista de Anza (1775-1776); the Mormon Battalion (1846-1847); the road established by Col. James B. Leach (1857); and the course of the San Antonio - San Diego Stage route established by Skillman, Wasson, Birch et al. (1857).

In modern context, Ahnert (1973 and 2011) includes a detailed map of the Snively's Station (Gila City) area toward the south and west. That map, however, does not include the entire route to Yuma Crossing and Fort Yuma.

Talbot (1992) includes a detailed map of the immediate Snively's Station vicinity that clearly concurs with Ahnert and the route as outlined in this segment map. He also includes a detailed map of the Yuma Crossing area. Talbot clearly overlays those segments on his maps of the Mormon Battalion Route through the area. He also indicates this route as having been explored by John Russell Bartlett during his U.S. - Mexico Boundary Survey as of June, 1852.

Comparing one map to another, those maps clearly indicate a southerly drop immediately to the west of Snively's / Swiveller's / Gila City into a westerly course onward to Yuma Crossing, although there is a significant gap between the joining points of those detailed maps.

The Oregon - California Trails Association (OCTA) has also done some field research and mapping of this segment. That data, supplied by Chris Wray of OCTA as of October 28, 2010, has also been taken into account. The detailed Wray / OCTA mapping data clearly indicates the same route as detailed by Ahnert, but it is sparse regarding the further westward segment to Yuma Crossing (which they identify correctly as "Jaeger Ferry").

Portions of this segment can be found on some modern maps identified as "Route of the Butterfield Stage" to the point at which it enters the broad plain approaching what is now Yuma. That terminus is in the vicinity of what is now S Madonna Road at State Highway 95 and appears to be the same terminus used by the Wray / OCTA and Ahnert maps.

Thereafter, the Butterfield Route appears to skirt various tributaries of the Colorado River on an essentially westerly track along a meandering course toward a brief northwesterly approach to Yuma Crossing.

The Butterfield entered California by way of Yuma Crossing / Jaeger's Ferry at the Colorado River from Arizona to Fort Yuma in California.

Talbot reports the Butterfield coaches "crossed the Colorado River on a ferry operated by Louis J.F. Yager (or Jaeger) at a cost of five dollars for a four-horse team."

Ormsby specifically mentions Mr. "Yager" and his ferry, noting that "The boat is a sort of flatboat, and is propelled by the rapid current, being kept on its course by pulleys running on a rope stretched across the river."

Yuma Crossing / Yager's Ferry / Jaeger's Ferry was located in the vicinity of what is now Yuma Crossing State Historical Park / Yuma Quartermaster Depot State Historic Park (Arizona - approximate coordinates N32° 43' 32.27", W114° 37' 19.42").

The Wray / OCTA mapping data places "Jaeger Ferry" at coordinates N32° 43' 42.16", W114° 37' 02.42" -- slightly east of the Quartermaster Depot State Park on the modern Kumeyaay Highway / Interstate 8.

The Yuma Crossing State Historical Park / Yuma Quartermaster Depot State Historic Park main office and visitor center is located at 201 N. 4th Avenue, Yuma, and is the site of several buildings and displays from the old Army Quartermasters' post established here. According to information from the Arizona State Parks:

> ... supplies were unloaded near the stone reservoir just west of the commanding officer's quarters and hauled up on a track running from the river dock through the center of the storehouse. They were shipped north on river steamers and overland by mule drawn freight wagons. The depot quartered up to 900 mules and a crew of teamsters to handle them. The Southern Pacific Railroad reached Yuma in 1877 and heralded the end of the Quartermaster Depot and Fort Yuma. The railroad reached Tucson in 1880, and the functions were moved to Fort Lowell in Tucson.
>
> The Signal Corps established a telegraph and weather station here in 1875. The supply depot was terminated by the Army in 1883, and the

pumps, steam engines and equipment were sent to Fort Lowell near Tucson, but the Signal Corps remained until 1891. The U.S. Weather Service was established as a separate agency and operated at the depot site until 1949.

The Yuma Crossing Quartermaster's Depot is listed on the National Register of Historic Places (Yuma Crossing and Associated Sites; 1966 - #66000197).

According to the National Register documentation, "First used by Native Americans, this natural crossing served as a significant transportation gateway on the Colorado River during the Spanish Colonial and U.S. westward expansion periods. The surviving buildings of the Yuma Quartermaster Depot and Arizona Territorial Prison are the key features on the Arizona side of the border; across the river, in California, stand the surviving buildings of Fort Yuma, an Army outpost that guarded the crossing from 1850 to 1885."

The next station location is at the original site of "Camp Yuma," later improved to become Fort Yuma near coordinates (N32° 43' 54.17", W114° 36' 55.83").

Ormsby specifically mentions Fort Yuma. Bailey lists Fort Yuma as a mileage point.

Information from the California State Military Department, California State Military Museum, reports that Fort Yuma was

First established on November 27, 1850, it was originally located in the bottoms near the Colorado River, less than a mile below the mouth of the Gila. In March 1851 the post was moved to a small elevation on the Colorado's west bank, opposite the present city of Yuma, Arizona, on the site of the former Mission Puerto de la Purísima Concepción. This site had been occupied by Camp Calhoun, named for John C. Calhoun, established on October 2, 1849, by 1st lieutenant Cave J. Couts, 1st Dragoons, for the boundary survey party led by 2nd Lieutenant Amiel W. Whipple, Corps of Topographical Engineers. A ferry service, maintained by the soldiers for the survey party's convenience, also accommodated emigrants. Fort Yuma was established to protect the southern emigrant travel route to California and to attempt control of the warlike Yuma Indians in the surrounding 100 mile area.

Established by Captain Samuel P. Heintzelman, 2nd Infantry, it was originally named Camp Independence. In March 1851, when the post was moved to its permanent site, its name was changed to Camp Yuma. A year later the post was designated Fort Yuma. In June 1851 the Army virtually abandoned the post because of the high costs incurred in maintaining it, and it was completely abandoned on December 6, 1851, when its commissary was practically empty of provisions.

The post, however, was reoccupied by Captain Heintzelman on February 29, 1852. In 1864 the Quartermaster Corps erected a depot on the left bank of the Colorado, below the mouth of the Gila River. When the extension of the railroad system obviated the need of a supply depot, Fort Yuma was abandoned on May 16, 1883. The reservation was transferred to the Interior Department on July 22, 1884. Today, the site of the military reservation is occupied by the Fort Yuma Indian School and a mission.

There are two historical markers of note located at the Butterfield period site of Fort Yuma near present-day 350 Picacho Road in Winterhaven, California.

The first is a California State Historical Marker (#806). It tells us "Fort Yuma - Originally called Camp Calhoun, the site was first used as a U.S. military post in 1849. A fire destroyed the original buildings. By 1855 the barracks had been rebuilt. Called Camp Yuma in 1852, it became Fort Yuma after reconstruction. Transferred to the Department of the Interior and the Quechan Indian Tribe in 1884, it became a boarding school operated by the Catholic Church until 1900."

The second relevant State Historical Resources Commission Marker (#350) recognizes the original Mission site. It reads "Mission La Purísima Concepción (Site of) - In October 1780, Father Francisco Garcés and companions began Mission La Purísima Concepción. The mission/pueblo site was inadequately supported. Colonists ignored Indian rights, usurped the best lands, and destroyed Indian crops. Completely frustrated and disappointed, the Quechans (Yumas) and their allies destroyed Concepción on July 17-19, 1781."

This marker is near the Saint Thomas Indian Mission, still a church and Catholic Services location serving the local Native American population. Information from the Diocese of San Diego, which administers the Mission, notes "The first mission at Ft. Yuma was named Purísima Concepción, established in 1780. It became a U.S. military outpost in the 19th century and was revived as an active mission again in 1919. The current church, St. Thomas Indian Mission, was dedicated in 1923."

The Ahnert, Talbot and Wray / OCTA data terminates at Yuma Crossing Arizona and does not include specifics regarding Fort Yuma in California.

References:

Arizona State Parks; *Yuma Quartermaster Depot State Historic Park*; Internet publication accessible at http://azstateparks.com/parks/YUQU/index.html (accessed August 8, 2010)

Bailey, Goddard; *California -- Arrival of the Overland Mail -- Itinerary of the Route*; as reported by newspaper article; *New York Times* (NY) - October 14, 1858.

Bailey, Goddard; *Report to Postmaster General A.V. Brown - Full itinerary as reported by De Bow's Review and Industrial Resources, Statistics etc.;* published by *De Bow's Review*; New Orleans and Washington City; 1858. See specifically *Internal Improvements - 1. Wagon Road to the Pacific*; pp. 719-721. Internet accessible at http://books.google.com/books?id=5CYoAAAAYAAJ&pg=PA720&lpg=PA720& dq=Cienega+de+los+Pimas&source=bl&ots=_5lZw_Bq23&sig=T6scCb8cpbY7K wjxpYoNvZpcgvI&hl=en&ei=i6KnS6KNOIr2M5yprIED&sa=X&oi=book_result& ct=result&resnum=2&ved=0CAwQ6AEwAQ#v=onepage&q=Cienega%20de%20 los%20Pimas&f=false (accessed March 22, 2010).

California State Military Department; *Fort Yuma (Including Camp Calhoun, Camp Independence, Camp Yuma, Yuma Quartermaster Depot)*; Internet publication accessible at http://www.militarymuseum.org/FtYuma.html (accessed August 8, 2010).

California State Parks - Office of Historic Preservation; *California Historical Landmarks*; Internet database - http://www.parks.ca.gov/default.asp?page_id=21387 (accessed April 4, 2010).

Conkling, Roscoe P. and Margaret B.; *The Butterfield Overland Mail, 1857– 1869* (3 vols.); Glendale, CA: A. H. Clark Company, 1947.

National Park Service; *Juan Bautista de Anza National Historic Trail Guide, Yuma County AZ*; Internet publication available at http://www.solideas.com/DeAnza/TrailGuide/ (accessed July 28, 2010).

National Park Service; *Juan Bautista de Anza National Historic Trail Guide, Imperial County CA*; Internet publication available at http://www.solideas.com/DeAnza/TrailGuide/ (accessed July 28, 2010).

National Register of Historic Places; *National Register Locations by State*; Internet publication; accessible at

174

http://www.nationalregisterofhistoricplaces.com/state.html (accessed May 3, 2010).

Oregon - California Trails Association; *Learn. Connect. Preserve.*; Internet publication accessible at http://www.octa-trails.org/ (accessed October 9, 2010).

Ormsby, Waterman L.; *The Butterfield Overland Mail (Only Through Passenger on the First Westbound Stage)*; original publications *New York Herald* (NY) Sep 26 - Nov 19, 1858; republished by Henry E. Huntington Library and Art Gallery, San Marino CA, 1942 – 1998.

Talbot, Dan; *Historical Guide to the Mormon Battalion and Butterfield Trail;* Westernlore Press, 1992.

FORT YUMA COLORADO RIVª CALª

**Historical lithograph of Fort Yuma 1875.
Litho by George Baker.**

ABOUT THE AUTHOR

Kirby Sanders is a career journalist, writer and historical researcher originally from Houston, Texas, and presently living in Northwest Arkansas. His writing endeavors have included poetry, short fiction, journalism and historical research reports.

During the late 1960s through the 1980s, he was active in the Southern Seed Poets Guild and Poets' Workshop literary groups in Houston. During that time he published several collections of poetry and edited several small literary journals. He also assisted in literary projects with Wings Press of Houston.

Among his early writing credits was publication in *From Hide and Horn, A Sesquicentennial Anthology of Texas Poets* published by Eakin Press of Austin, Texas, in 1986 wherein 150 Texas writers were selected to write a work encapsulating one year in Texas history.

In the early 1970s, he was employed as a writer and reporter with the *Houston (TX) Chronicle*. During the 1980s, he branched out into travel and tourism writing. During the 1990s he returned to daily journalism and worked at newspapers in East Texas and Northwest Arkansas.

During that time, he received several awards for investigative reporting. Amongst those was a substantial series on the arrest of the final suspect in the 1963 Sixteenth Street Baptist Church bombing in Birmingham, Alabama -- the infamous "Four Little Girls" murder case.

Many of his feature stories during that time focused on the history of the communities in which he worked. He has also worked in film, radio and television.

In 2011, he was selected as a consultant to the National Park Service to prepare a substantial report and mapping survey on the 1858-1861 Butterfield Overland Mail stagecoach route in the states of Missouri, Arkansas, Oklahoma, Texas, New Mexico, Arizona and California.

He has also authored two novels, *A Death In Texas* and *Nusquam Res, Nusquam Esse; the Final Journey of Ambrose Bierce.*

Made in the USA
Las Vegas, NV
29 November 2023

81827502R00112